BRIDGING THE GAPS

Public Pension Funds and
Infrastructure Finance

Clive Lipshitz & Ingo Walter

Authors: Lipshitz, Clive and Walter, Ingo
Title: Bridging the Gaps: Public Pension Funds and
Infrastructure Finance
ISBN: 9781077442368

Preface

America faces two public finance challenges that – if left unaddressed – will have serious implications for the fiscal stability of state and local governments and for the quality of life of all Americans. The funded status of public pension plans and the state of the country's critical infrastructure are generally viewed as distinct subjects. This book argues otherwise. Over the long term, when one deteriorates, the other is sure to follow. Moreover, infrastructure investments are well suited to the portfolio needs of public pension plans, which in turn comprise the single largest pool of capital untapped for the financing needs of American infrastructure.

Confronting America's infrastructure gap is one of the few national issues with bipartisan political support. It is a priority for the American public and for elected officials at the federal, state, and local levels. Any debate on solutions to close the $2 trillion 10-year investment gap quickly focuses on funding – revenue streams in the form of dedicated taxes or user fees – and financing solutions. The tax-exempt municipal bond market is a uniquely American creation. In spite of that source of financing, the infrastructure gap persists. At the same time, there is $4.3 trillion of untapped capital in the portfolios of public pension plans.

Infrastructure assets have features that are appealing to pension investors. They are of long-duration and offer some degree of protection against inflation. They are uncorrelated with other asset classes, so they offer much-needed diversification. Best of all, they generate steady cash flows to meet the needs of current retirees. Yet, the infrastructure investment programs of the big American public pension plans are relatively new and modestly sized – averaging about 1% of fund assets, compared for example with allocations of 5% to 10% that are typical of similarly sized Canadian pension plans.

There is another issue. When pensions invest in infrastructure, they generally use private equity-type funds that often benefit from first-rate expertise but are oriented to achieving capital gains, not the current income that supports payments to pension beneficiaries.

We begin with a comprehensive introduction to the public pension system, drawing on a primary dataset comprising thousands of observations drawn from a decade of annual reports of the 25 largest public pension systems (these account for 55% of all public pension assets in the country). We offer recommendations for enhancing pension governance and suggest ways in which pensions can obtain greater control over their investment programs and expenses.

We explore how pension plans invest in infrastructure and how that asset class has performed, particularly relative to other investment options. We find that most pension plan investing in U.S. infrastructure is allocated to secondary transactions in privately-held assets, although infrastructure financing needs are most acute in paying for the operation and maintenance of existing public infrastructure and in greenfield development.

Taking a prescriptive approach, we investigate ways to better match pension capital to infrastructure investment needs, without compromising the fiduciary duties of pension trustees. We illustrate how the infrastructure asset class might grow and evolve as the needs of capital providers and capital users converge. This should, we believe, lead to solutions that benefit both public infrastructure and the needs of public pension systems. For inspiration, we look at innovative financing solutions, the role of EPC (engineering, procurement, and construction) firms, and models that have been successful in countries such as Canada and Australia.

It is our hope that this book provides transparency to complex public finance challenges, and presents a range of ideas that can be explored by responsible officials and policymakers. We also hope that advisors and investors find much of value in this book. Ultimately, it is our objective for this book to provide a positive contribution to the search for solutions to the persistent gaps facing America's public pension system, as well as a range of ideas for unlocking capital to reduce America's persistent infrastructure gap, thereby creating winners on both ends of the financial chain.

We are indebted to Jean-Pierre Aubry, Joe Azelby, John Biggs, Sussan Corson, Leo De Bever, Jameson Doig, Arpit Gupta, James Harkness, Allan Ickowitz, Michael Kahn, Todd Kanaster, Hank Kim, Peter Mixon, Yuliya Oryol, Paul Rosenstiel, Dave Russ, Gus Schwed, Thomas Shevlin, Patrick Springer, Todd Tauzer, Stijn Van Niewerburgh, Mark Weisdorf and several others for helpful comments on earlier versions of this study. Patricio Cox and Lebogang Mahlare from the Tandon School of Engineering provided invaluable research assistance in developing our dataset from primary sources and Fernando Falbo, an incoming Fulbright Scholar in Economics, was instrumental in preparing this volume for publication. The authors alone are responsible for any errors of fact, omission or interpretation.

We gratefully acknowledge financial support from the New York University Global Institute for Advanced Study through the Infrastructure Finance Initiative at the Stern School of Business.

Clive Lipshitz
Ingo Walter
New York City, July 2019

Contents

List of Figures

List of Tables

1
Introduction

The U.S. public pension system comprises 297 distinct state systems and 5,232 local systems[1] with aggregate assets of \$4.33 trillion[2] held in trust to fund future pension benefits accrued at the end of 2017 for the 20.6 million employees of state, county, and city governments. Pension obligations at the end of 2017 were estimated at \$5.96 trillion,[2] indicating a funding gap of \$1.63 trillion. That is, U.S. pension systems covering all public employees except those of the federal government on average showed a "funded ratio" of 72.6%.[3]

Public pension plans invest in diversified portfolios of assets, usually with some degree of matching to the long duration of pension liabilities. Among the asset classes in which public pension systems invest, infrastructure is one that has received growing attention in recent years because of key direct and indirect benefits it is thought to provide to pension portfolios.

---

[1]National pension membership data taken from Annual Survey of Public Pensions 2017, United States Census Bureau: https://www.census.gov/data/tables/2017/econ/aspp/aspp-historical-tables.html.

[2]National pension asset and liability statistics taken from Financial Accounts of the United States: Flow of Funds, Balance Sheets and Integrated Macroeconomic Accounts, Board of Governors of the Federal Reserve System, Fourth Quarter 2017, page 99: https://www.federalreserve.gov/releases/z1/20180308/z1.pdf.

[3]The funded ratio represents the ratio of plan assets to pension liabilities. We use the market value of plan assets as the numerator and accrued actuarial liabilities as the denominator in this ratio.

In this study, we analyze the U.S. public pension system using a ten-year dataset for each of the 25 largest public pension plans which in aggregate represent 55% of public pension assets in the country. We explore the role of infrastructure investing in the portfolios of these plans and examine how infrastructure has performed as an asset class relative to the performance parameters sought by pension system trustees. Based on our findings, we suggest a number of initiatives for enhanced governance of public pension systems as well as more effective long-term models for financial intermediation between investment managers and public pension systems. Some of our observations apply to other types of institutional investors such as insurance companies, corporate pension plans, and sovereign wealth funds. To provide context, we begin with an overview of the U.S. public pension system.

1.1 An Overview of the U.S. Public Pension System

Unlike in the private sector, where defined contribution retirement plans have become the norm, public sector employees[4] generally participate in employer-sponsored defined benefit plans. This is a primary attraction for public sector employment and conveys substantial benefits for retirement security.[5]

---

[4]We use the term "public sector employees" to denote all public sector workers except those employed by the federal government and its entities – i.e., employees of states, municipalities, and special districts funded by local tax and services revenues and local borrowing capacity.

[5]Participation in these plans is almost always mandatory. The vesting period for pension participants is generally 5-10 years. See Table A4 in Mattoon (2007) for a state-by-state detail of vesting periods. While vesting disincentivizes labor mobility, there are restricted reciprocity agreements between certain retirement systems, for example those within California.

Public pension systems fund benefit payments from three sources: Contributions from employees,[6] contributions from employers,[7] and investment gains and income from assets held in investment portfolios. As public pension systems have matured, the last of these sources has come to provide the bulk of cash flows.[8] This trend is likely to become more pronounced going forward.[9] Almost all public pension systems are today in a negative cash-flow position, with benefit payments exceeding contributions. This places significant pressure on the performance of investment portfolios intended to fund future pension liabilities.[10]

The employer contribution is calculated by actuaries to cover the "normal cost" of benefits accrued in the current year[11] as

---

[6]Generally, in the range of 5-10% of wages, see Table A4 in Mattoon (2007). Contributions are generally higher for employees who do not participate in Social Security. About 25% of public sector employees do not participate in Social Security, see Table A3 in Mattoon (2007) for a state-by-state analysis

[7]Generally, 5-15%, see Table A4 in Mattoon (2007)

[8]U.S. Census Bureau Data compiled by the National Association of State Retirement Administrators (NASRA, 2018) indicates that over the period 1988-2017, investment earnings accounted for $4.68 trillion (62%) of public pension plan revenues, employer contributions accounted for $1.97 trillion (26%), and employee contributions for $0.89 trillion (12%).

[9]Munnell et al (2013) explain that this factor is particularly critical for mature plans where assets are large and cash flows are both negative and becoming more negative over time.

[10]This is not uniform for pension systems globally. Some countries have pay-as-you-go regimes, where current revenues fund current benefits. Indeed, this is how U.S. public sector employers fund other post-employment benefits (OPEB).

[11]Benefit accruals are determined by actuaries. They are based on periodic experience studies (usually undertaken every five years) pursuant to which underlying assumptions regarding factors such as mortality, compensation, and employment are revisited.

well as the cost of amortizing unfunded liabilities accrued in prior years.[12] It is referred to as the Actuarially Determined Employer Contribution (ADEC).[13] In order to avoid fluctuations in annual public sector budgets, public pension systems generally smooth the impact of investment gains and losses on their ADECs over a period of time, usually five years.[14]

The challenges facing public pension systems in the form of growing unfunded pension liabilities are well understood and documented. Their genesis is complex, and many of the contributing factors are beyond the control of those who oversee pension systems. The key factors include:

- Attributes of benefit and funding policy – notably historical decisions regarding the level of pension benefits, requirements for employee contributions, and fluctuations in employer contributions. All of these have contributed to the funding gap. Indeed, the credit rating agency S&P Global notes that "a consistent and sustainable commitment to funding seems to be the stronger indicator of overall health for the highest-funded plans".[15]

---

[12]Amortization is generally over a 20 to 30 year period.

[13]The actuarial standard pursuant to which actuaries calculate the ADEC is Actuarial Standard of Practice No. 27 (ASOP 27): https://www.actuarialstandardsboard.org/wp-content/uploads/2014/02/asop027_172.pdf. Section 3.6 of this Standard outlines the assumptions actuaries use in determining the ADEC, including inflation, investment returns, and other factors.

[14]Smoothing is accomplished by averaging market value of assets over a trailing period. The resultant rolling average asset level is referred to as the "actuarial value of assets." Public pension plan sponsors are not legally required, in most cases, to fund ADECs on an annual basis. As we shall illustrate, this is a fundamental cause of underfunding of many pension systems.

[15]Ososami and Tauzer (2017). Munnell et al (2015) illustrate how plan

- Demography – the ageing of the U.S. population and gathering wave of baby-boomer retirement have reduced, and will continue to reduce, the worker-to-beneficiary ratio. The retirement headwind will be reinforced in the longer-term as a result of lower U.S. fertility rates[16] in the absence of higher levels of immigration.

- Longevity – longer life spans lead to pension payouts that extend beyond the timeframe for which actuarial calculations were determined in prior periods.

- Interregional migration – population movements between regions of the United States have skewed the worker-to-beneficiary ratio in some cities and states.

- Capital market expectations – future investment returns may not match those achieved in the past decade. This has the dual effect of reducing future asset growth and increasing the present value of pension liabilities.

- The "echo effect" of the 2008 financial market turmoil – Brainard and Brown (2016) note that the U.S. public pension system lost 34.4% of its asset value during the Global Financial Crisis (GFC), with assets dropping from $3.2 trillion in 2007 to $2.1 trillion in 2009. The system has not fully recovered since that time.[17]

---

sponsors have tended to reduce contributions during years in which investment returns are particularly strong.

[16]Ely and Hamilton (2018) report that fertility in the United States fell between 2007 and 2017 by 18% in large metropolitan areas, 16% in small/medium metro areas, and 12% in rural areas.

[17]Prior to 2001, most pension systems were fully funded. Funded status began to weaken after the bear market in 2000 and this trend was substantially exacerbated as a result of the GFC. Despite strong market performance in recent years, funded status has continued to deteriorate as pension liabilities have grown faster than plan assets.

While the growth in unfunded pension liabilities can in large part be attributable to these factors, a more insidious element is the interest rate used to discount future pension obligations to present value.

Government Accounting Standards Board (GASB) rules provide that pension obligations be discounted using a rate that equals the expected investment return of a pension system's portfolio (with some exceptions).[18] Pension administrators adjust the

---

[18]GASB 67, introduced in 2015, requires that pension assets be reported at market value, not on a smoothed basis (previous accounting rules permitted assets to be valued using smoothing techniques, reducing the effect of prior-year market movements). GASB 67 also put restrictions on the exclusive use of expected returns in determining the discount rate, requiring instead that liabilities be measured partly on an expected-return basis (for the funded portion of liabilities) and partly on the basis of low-risk debt (for the unfunded portion). The assumption behind the unfunded portion is that it would have to be covered on a pay-as-you-go basis. Since most pension actuaries believe that pensions will remain funded, only 13 of 144 plans made use of the lower discount rate in a study using 2014 data by Weinberg and Norcross (2017). Corporate pension liabilities are discounted entirely on the basis of low-risk debt. GASB 68, which provides for the reporting of pension liabilities, permits pensions to continue using asset smoothing in the calculation of the ADEC. There is an active debate about the appropriateness of GASB methodology for calculating pension liabilities. One side of the debate, taken by financial economists, is that since pension liabilities are certain obligations, they should be discounted at close to a risk-free rate. This approach would discount liabilities using the yield on state general obligation debt and – if these obligations have higher priority than state debt – the rate of long-duration U.S. treasuries. The net effect would be a considerable ballooning in total pension obligations. See for example, Novy-Marx and Rauh (2010). Essentially, this approach seeks to value pension liabilities at a point in time based on how much a willing buyer would need to be paid to take on these liabilities. The other side of the debate relies on the argument that public pension systems are going concerns and their liabilities – as distinct from those of corporate pension plans – cannot easily be offset in the market. Rather, this side argues, pensions should be valued based on the future cost of funding. This is called the "level funding" approach. See Tauzer and Kanaster (2018) and Anson (2011). We follow the

discount rate based on expected future returns. There is clear evidence of discount rate reductions by almost all public pension systems, and it is possible that even today's more modest discount rates continue to reflect unrealistic expectations for future investment returns.

A lower funded ratio is not inherently problematic if the jurisdiction sponsoring the pension plan has a credible basis for expecting positive economic growth – growth that can be expected to result in favorable demographics (number of workers versus pension beneficiaries) and a growing general tax base.[19]

Ultimate responsibility for oversight of public pension systems rests with the plan fiduciary, which in most cases takes the form of a board of trustees.[20] In some cases, the board may have an investment committee tasked specifically with overseeing the system's investment program.[21]

Andonov et al (2017) categorize pension trustees into three groups – public sector representatives, general public representatives, and active or retired representatives of plan participants. The authors also categorize how trustees obtain their board seats – appointed, elected, or by virtue of public office ("ex officio").

GASB accounting methodology in this study.

[19]Mattoon (2007) argues that when growth in pension costs is below growth in the tax base, a funded ratio of less than 100 percent can be appropriate.

[20]In rare cases, such as with New York State and Local Retirement System and North Carolina Retirement System, there is a single fiduciary (the State Comptroller and State Treasurer, respectively).

[21]Non-investment responsibilities of the board include overseeing actuarial evaluations, setting benefit and contribution policy (ultimately enacted by a legislature), and overseeing administration of contributions and benefit payments.

Their analysis of the governance models of a large group of public pension systems is summarized in Table 1.1.

Table 1.1: Composition of Boards of Trustees of Public Pension Systems

		Means of Selection		
		Appointed	Ex-Officio	Elected
Type of Representative	State	7.56%[22]	25.40%[23]	1.31%
	Public	24.60%[24]	0.15%	0.77%
	Participant	11.53%[25]	1.69%	27.01%[26]

Source: Andonov et al (2017)[27]

Day-to-day oversight of pension fund investment programs is delegated to investment staff, under the leadership of a Chief Investment Officer (CIO). The CIO and plan fiduciary,[28] advised

---

[22]This group of trustees is usually appointed by the governor (in the case of a state pension system) or the mayor or county executive (in the case of a municipal system).

[23]These trustees are state or city officers, such as treasurers and comptrollers.

[24]Often, these trustees are from the financial services industry. In the sample presented in the study, only four pension systems had public representatives appointed by members, the rest were appointed by the sponsoring government entity.

[25]Trustees in this group are usually nominated by plan participants and appointed by a state official.

[26]These trustees are elected directly by plan participants.

[27]Data in this table is based on 1,185 trustees of 212 public pension plans and is weighted by the number of private equity investments held by each plan.

[28]Fiduciary standards for trustees of public pension plans are governed by state law and are different from rules that apply to trustees of corporate pension plans, which are governed by the Employee Retirement Income

by investment consultants, determine asset allocation, which is generally captured in an investment policy statement that sets out permissible ranges for each asset class within the overall portfolio.

Ultimately, pension liabilities are obligations of the respective public sector employer (i.e., taxpayers) to public sector employees. So funding issues have a direct impact on public finance. Credit rating agencies have increasingly considered the impact of unfunded pension liabilities on the creditworthiness of states and municipalities in issuing ratings. In extreme situations, seriously underfunded pension liabilities can become a fiscal burden on public finances as bonds are down-rated and interest rate spreads widen to reflect deteriorating prospects of interest and principal payments being made in full and on time. This scenario has not so far been a systemic issue in the United States as a whole, although it is heading in that direction in certain cities and states.[29]

In light of these generally adverse developments, what have public pension systems done to reduce unfunded liabilities?

Most have sought to close the funding gap through greater reliance on the performance of their investment portfolios. Fundamental is selecting the optimal asset allocation model.

Modern portfolio theory is well understood, as is its application to the pension sector. The key is to calibrate the impact of asset selection and rebalancing over economic and financial

---

Security Act (ERISA).

[29] A report by Fitch Ratings notes that pension funding is a more substantive concern for local than state governments, since labor costs represent a proportionately greater component of local government budgets. See Offerman et al (2011)

cycles on portfolio performance in the presence of risk parameters reflecting those of end-stakeholders – in this case pension beneficiaries and (ultimately) taxpayers. It is essential to align asset allocation to portfolio returns, risk targets, and correlations between asset classes. Then security and fund selection must be calibrated at the level of both asset managers and assets. Risk measurement for long-duration investors such as pension systems is best done with long-term measures rather than relying on monthly or quarterly risk parameters.

Innovation is as fundamental to portfolio management as it is to other disciplines. This entails being informed of emerging asset classes – including infrastructure – and having the capabilities to evaluate investments in these areas. Where such capabilities do not exist internally, they should be sourced from outside experts.

In the early 2000s, U.S. pension systems began adopting allocations to hedge funds, which appeared to provide strong risk-adjusted returns. Over time, this approach proved to be of limited benefit due to widespread underperformance of hedge funds, as well as the certainty of high fees. As a consequence, many U.S. public pension systems substantially reduced or eliminated these allocations.

Instead, they turned increasingly to private equity, credit, and real assets (real estate, infrastructure, and natural resources). These longer-duration investments provided a better match to the long duration of pension liabilities, access to illiquidity premia, and (in the case of credit and real assets) current cash flows to help ameliorate near-term cash needs to pay ongoing pension benefits. As pension systems continued to mature, they would have had to reduce the degree of illiquidity in their portfolios, thereby forgoing illiquidity premia and potentially exacerbating any funding gaps.

Net investment returns are what drive portfolio performance. Nevertheless, there is an increased focus on the spread between gross and net investment returns in the form of investment expenses. This begins with transparency, and fee disclosure by pension systems is surprisingly opaque. Pension systems generally report investment management fees, consulting fees, and other related expenses, although even this information is disclosed inconsistently between pension systems. Very few pension systems disclose performance fees and "carried interest"[30] which often constitute the largest portion of expenses associated with alternative investment allocations such as private equity funds.[31] Nor do most pension systems disclose the internal costs of managing their portfolios – i.e. the compensation and related costs of their own investing teams.[32] This opacity is unhelpful in assessing pension plan governance. It has led to pressure for greater fee transparency and to reign in what are believed to be excessive investment expenses. There are structural impediments to adequate transparency as many pension systems simply do not obtain the requisite data from the investment managers to which they allocate capital.[33] Additionally, there is a perception

---

[30]Carried interest is the contractual right of the general partner of a fund to a percentage of investment profits.

[31]An exception, with very good disclosure is New York State and Local Retirement System, which provides an auxiliary schedule of all of its management fees and performance-related investment expenses. Teacher Retirement System of Texas also provides good expense disclosure. California Government Code Section 7514.7 mandates disclosure of fees, expenses, and carried interest for capital commitments by the state's pension systems to alternative investment funds made on or after January 1, 2017 and the two large California pension systems have begun providing detailed disclosure of their investment expenses.

[32]Some pension systems disclose the annual budget of their administration organization, which includes the cost of internal investment staff. Overall, this disclosure is very limited.

[33]The Institutional Limited Partners Association (ILPA), a trade body

of resistance on the part of pension investment staff to pressure
investment managers on fund fees in order to avoid losing access
to preferred managers. Expense disclosure has taken on a life
of its own in the eyes of both plan sponsors and plan participants.[34] In a 2017 report, the American Federation of Teachers put forward several recommendations to address this issue
as it pertains to the management of teacher pensions, including
reallocation from the most expensive fund managers (particularly funds-of-funds), instituting policies and legislation requiring more complete fee disclosure, and negotiation of fee limits.[35]
The report asserted that fees remained excessive because of "the
culture among pension funds, promulgated by consultants and
investment managers, that promotes acting in isolation from –
and often in competition with – other pension funds on the question of fees."[36]

---

representing institutional investors in private equity, has made fee disclosure
one of its primary areas of focus.

[34]See Flood, C. (2018, July 8). Pennsylvania State Treasurer Condemns
$5.5 billion fee 'waste'. *Financial Times*. Elsewhere, we discuss a report
commissioned in Pennsylvania to disclose details on investment expenses.
We also discuss an expense report commissioned by the California State
Teachers' Retirement System. Narrative in these reports illustrates complexities associated with obtaining expense data.

[35]Specifically, to management fees of 0.9% and carried interest of 9%.
The report estimated that with these limits, a sample of 12 public pension
plans with an aggregate $787 billion in assets could have saved $1.8 billion
over five years relative to the $35.5 billion in fees that the report estimated
these plans paid over that period (assuming a 7% gross investment return).

[36]AFT (2017). The study has some provocative assertions such as a
quote from a Washington Post article that "the top 25 hedge fund managers
earned more in 2015 than all of the kindergarten teachers in the U.S. combined" and commentary that "alternative investment management fees are
a main contributor to the pension funding crisis... Our recommendations
call on pension fund staff and trustees to take specific steps to reduce the
current excessive alternative fee structure in order to reverse the transfer
of wealth from middle-class workers and their retirement savings to Wall

Some underfunded pension systems have adopted a temporary fix involving a cash infusion via issuance of "pension bonds".[37] These may be viewed as an attempted arbitrage between interest payments due and the investment returns that the plan sponsor believes will eventually be earned on bond proceeds.[38]

In the decade following the GFC, many states and municipalities instituted reforms to reduce the funding gap in their pension systems. Brainard and Brown (2016) note that the market-driven increase in the pension-funding gap during that period led to an automatic increase in employer contributions at the very time that tax revenues were substantially impaired due to the financial crisis. They outline a series of pension system reforms implemented by state governments between 2007 and 2015 – specifics that depend on the particularities of each state's legal framework.[39]

Because of legal constraints on adjusting pension terms for ex-

---

Street billionaires" as well as "alternative investments, due to their high fee structures, serve to siphon money directly out of pension funds into the hands of asset managers."

[37]Pension obligation bonds are bonds (often not tax-exempt) issued by governments to address pension funding gaps.

[38]In a volatile market environment, these are risky structures as the intended arbitrage may not materialize. Moreover, they convert the "soft" liability of a pension obligation into the "hard" liability of debt service, affecting the borrowing capacity of the government entity. A governance issue associated with pension bonds occurs if proceeds from the bond sale are used for purposes other than pension funding. Mattoon (2007) illustrates that Illinois issued $10 billion of pension bonds in 2003, of which $2.7 billion was used to fund general budget purposes and not for funding pension plan obligations.

[39]The authors provide a detailed state-by-state analysis of reforms.

isting employees,[40] much of the burden of reform during the post-crisis period fell on new hires. Employee contributions were increased in 36 states, adjustments were made to benefit-calculation formulas in several states, nine states increased the vesting period for pension eligibility, and five states created hybrid plans for new hires with a mixture of defined benefit and defined contribution features.[41] Unsurprisingly, because of the many constraints on pension reform,[42] these actions led to litigation in about half of the affected states.

It is possible that in extreme circumstances, eligible municipalities unable to fund pension obligations may have the option of restructuring through a bankruptcy proceeding, although this is likely to be a disputed issue. This option is unavailable to states. Beermann (2012) notes that state law and the Contract Clause of the U.S. Constitution may preclude states from enacting meaningful pension reform, and that the Constitution may demand complete payment of all pension obligations even if a state is insolvent".[43]

---

[40]Mattoon (2007) discusses legal restrictions on benefit adjustments which in approximately 40 states are constrained by non-impairment clauses in state constitutions or in statutes governing pension systems. The Contracts Clause and the Takings Clause of the U.S. Constitution are also relied upon to defend pension rights.

[41]One of the best funded pension systems – the Wisconsin Retirement System – has a risk-sharing feature whereby plan members absorb market losses, a feature akin to the structure of defined contribution plans.

[42]Monahan (2013) provides a detailed outline of the legal constraints that apply to pension reform.

[43]The author outlines in detail the constitutional and legal protections afforded pension benefits and describes practices dating back to the 1970s that he believes led to the current challenges facing the U.S. public pension system, including pension "spiking," decisions by politicians to promise deferred compensation that would not impact current year budgets but would win support from unions, taxpayer indifference, the reliance on overly optimistic

To reiterate, the assumption behind the public pension system is that pension obligations are inviolable obligations of the plan sponsor, essentially providing the pension system with something akin to a put option against the plan sponsor and those funding its obligations, i.e. taxpayers. It is for this reason that this subject is of more than casual significance to the general public.

Building on this discussion, we can reduce the issue of pension funding to the following six expressions:

i $UAAL = AAL - MVA$[44]

ii $AAL = f($Pension Obligations, Discount Rate$)$

iii Discount Rate $= f($Expected Rate of Return, Municipal Bond Rate$)$

iv Expected Rate of Return $= f($Asset Allocation, Security Selection, Correlation, Portfolio Risk, Capital Market Performance, Inflation, Investment Expenses$)$

v $MVA(i) = MVA(i-1) + ADEC$ x Percentage Contributed + Employee Contributions + Investment Gains and Income − Benefit Payments + Adjustments[45]

---

projected rates of return, and "in some states and localities, corruption." The author also addresses the moral hazard and complexity associated with any consideration of a federal bailout of public pension plans and OPEB.

[44]Where UAAL is Unfunded Actuarial Accrued Liability, AAL is Actuarial Accrued Liability, and MVA is Market Value of Assets. GASB accounting replaces UAAL with Net Pension Liability (NPL) and MVA with Plan Fiduciary Net Position (PFNP).

[45]This is represented in pension financial reporting by the Statement of Changes in Net Position.

vi $ADEC = f($Normal Cost + Amortization of prior period $UAAL)$

Very few of the factors in these expressions are within the control of investment staff who administer pension systems. We shall return to this issue later in our study.

2
Focus on the Largest U.S. Public Pension Systems

We now turn to an analysis of the factors discussed in our overview of the public pension system using a dataset covering the twenty-five largest public pension systems in the United States.[46] While many pension studies use the Public Plans Database maintained by the Center for Retirement Research at Boston College, our dataset relies directly on the annual financial reports and other filings of the 25 pension systems. We include in our analysis a number of data fields not maintained by the Public Plans Database and extend our analysis beyond already available time-series.

Our dataset comprises ten years ending with the 2017 fiscal year, covering data from 250 distinct annual reports. Of the 25 plans in our study, 22 are sponsored by state governments with the remaining three sponsored by the governments of New York City[47] and Los Angeles County. In aggregate, the 25 plans man-

---

[46]The selection of this sample is based on the 2017 ranking of public pension systems published by the National Association of State Retirement Systems: https://www.nasra.org/Files/Public%20Fund%20Survey/AppendixA.pdf.

[47]While collectively managed by the New York City Bureau of Asset Management, the City's five pension systems have distinct liability streams and are overseen by separate boards of trustees, which is why they are accounted for on a disaggregated basis. Combined, they would be the fourth

age $2.38 trillion in assets for 16.9 million members, and have liabilities of $3.12 trillion (as at the end of fiscal 2017). They account for 55% of total plan assets and 53.5% of plan liabilities of the entire U.S. public pension system.

Table 2.1 provides key summary statistics for each of these plans, while Figure 2.1 graphically orders the pension plans by market value of assets.

---

largest pension system in the country, with $182 billion in assets as at June 30, 2017.

Table 2.1: The 25 Largest Public Pension Systems in the United States at Year-end 2017

Pension System	Acronym	Plan Assets at Market Value ($mm)	Actuarial Liabilties ($mm)	Funding Gap at Market Value ($ mm)	Funded Status at Market Value (%)	Total Plan Members	Fiscal Year End
California Public Employees Retirement System	CalPERS	326.406	465.046	138.640	70.2%	1.925.459	Jun 30
California State Teachers Retirement System	CalSTRS	208.700	286.950	78.250	72.7%	933.301	Jun 30
New York State and Local Retirement System	NYSLRS	197.359	209.992	12.633	94.0%	1.104.779	Mar 31
Florida Retirement System	FRS	153.573	178.600	25.027	86.0%	1.193.637	Jun 30
Teacher Retirement System of Texas	TexasTRS	146.127	181.753	35.626	80.4%	1.545.057	Aug 31
New York State Teachers Retirement System	NYSTRS	115.468	115.672	204	99.8%	428.579	Jun 30
Wisconsin Retirement System	WRS	104.574	100.819	(3.755)	103.7%	632.802	Dec 31
North Carolina Retirement Systems	NCRS	93.534	105.927	12.393	88.3%	1.003.139	Jun 30
Ohio Public Employees Retirement System	ERSOhio	86.586	102.274	15.688	84.7%	1.091.957	Dec 31
Washington Department of Retirement Systems	WDRS	84.853	92.791	7.938	91.4%	558.838	Jun 30
New Jersey Division of Pension and Benefits	NJDPB	79.312	158.863	79.551	49.9%	758.845	Jun 30
Virginia Retirement System	VRS	72.814	93.501	20.687	77.9%	687.818	Jun 30
Georgia Teachers Retirement System	GTRS	71.341	89.926	18.585	79.3%	352.843	Jun 30
Ohio State Teachers Retirement System	OSTRS	71.119	96.126	25.008	74.0%	465.704	Jun 30
Oregon Employees Retirement System	OERS	66.372	77.094	10.722	86.1%	355.449	Jun 30
New York City Employees Retirement System	NYCERS	60.784	82.421	21.637	73.7%	414.226	Jun 30
Pennsylvania Public School Employees Retirement System	PSERS	52.937	101.972	49.035	51.9%	485.959	Jun 30
Los Angeles County Employees Retirement Association	LACERA	52.744	66.012	13.268	79.9%	160.516	Jun 30
Michigan Public School Employees Retirement System	MPSERS	52.566	76.700	24.134	68.5%	435.974	Sep 30
New York City Teachers Retirement System	NYCTRS	50.096	73.323	23.227	68.3%	207.000	Jun 30
Illinois Teachers Retirement System	ILTRS	49.376	122.904	73.528	40.2%	412.451	Jun 30
Maryland State Retirement and Pension System	MSRPS	48.987	69.987	20.999	70.0%	402.736	Jun 30
Colorado Public Employees Retirement Association	ColPera	48.639	74.389	25.750	65.4%	584.070	Jun 30
Tennessee Consolidated Retirement System	TCRS	46.239	48.856	2.617	94.6%	523.940	Jun 30
Missouri Public Schools Retirement System	MPSRS	41.727	49.711	7.984	83.9%	250.036	Jun 30
Aggregate		2.382.231	3.121.610	739.378	77.4%	16.915.115	

Source: Comprehensive Annual Financial Reports. Public pension systems report actuarial liabilities with a one-year lag such that liabilities reported in 2017 annual reports are typically those for 2016. In order to present a more up-to-date analysis, we have used 2017 liabilities – sourced from 2017 actuarial reports and 2018 comprehensive annual financial reports, where available. We report funded status as the ratio of market value of assets to pension liabilities (other studies use actuarially smoothed assets in the numerator). As a result of these factors, the funding gap and funded status reported here are different from those reported by the pension systems in their 2017 annual reports. Most, but not all, public pension systems have a June fiscal year end. Because it is not possible to obtain intra-year data on most metrics analyzed in this study, we have made a simplifying assumption and used actual fiscal year end for all plans. This has a minor effect on comparability across pension systems. All data herein is as at the end of the respective fiscal year, unless otherwise noted.

Figure 2.1: **Plan Assets of 25 Largest Public Pension Systems (\$ billion, 2017)**

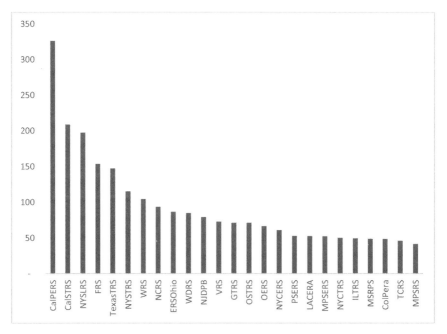

Source: Comprehensive Annual Financial Reports. Plan assets are reported at market value.

We turn now to an analysis of these pension systems, focusing on the respective factors addressed in the introduction – funding sources, discipline in funding employer pension contributions, pension liabilities and funded status, the discount rate, the impact of demographics, benefit levels, asset allocation, investment performance, and investment expenses.

2.1 Funding Sources

As discussed earlier, pension systems are funded from three sources: Contributions by plan members, contributions by employers, and return on plan invested assets. Over the ten-year period ending

2017, investment returns contributed $1.4 trillion (66.0%) of total funding of the 25 plans, employer contributions accounted for $462 billion (22.5%) and employee contributions accounted for $236 billion (11.5%).[48] See Figure 2.2 for aggregate data and Figure 2.3 for annual data.

The extent to which pension plans rely on returns from their investment portfolios highlights the importance of investment performance for cash flow projections modeled by pension administrators. This observation is particularly pertinent in the case of mature plans with large accumulated asset pools. Downside risk from market volatility can be substantial – aggregate losses for the 25 public pension systems during the GFC were $117 billion in 2008 and an additional $323 billion in 2009.

---

[48]This breakdown is very similar to the 20-year data cited in NASRA, 2018.

Figure 2.2: **Aggregate Cash Flows of 25 Largest Public Pension Systems ($ billion, 2008-2017)**

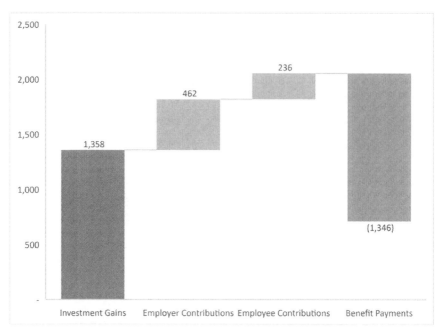

Source: Comprehensive Annual Financial Reports.

Figure 2.3: **Annual Cash Flows of 25 Largest Public Pension Systems ($ billion, 2008-2017)**

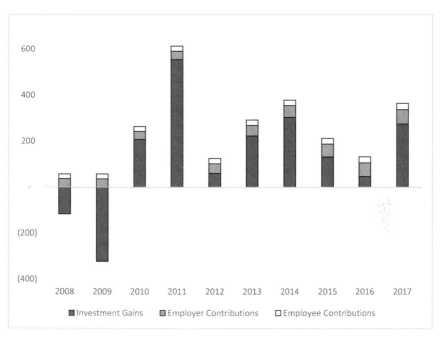

Source: Comprehensive Annual Financial Reports.

2.2 Discipline in Funding of Employer Contributions

As noted, discipline in funding the actuarially-determined employer contribution, or ADEC, is a cornerstone of sound pension administration. Certain pension systems routinely fund the entire employer contribution. Six pension systems in our dataset exhibit perfect records over the entire period captured by the Public Plans Database (2001-2017 for most pension systems). Sponsors of a small number of pension systems routinely under-fund employer contributions.[49] While ADEC funding discipline is only one component in explaining the financial condition of public pension systems, a causative relationship is suggested in Figure 2.4. Pension systems with a lower percentage of ADEC funded (towards the left of the x-axis) also tend to have lower overall funded status (lower on the y-axis). Nevertheless, the cluster of data-points on the far right of the chart illustrates that ADEC funding alone does not determine funded status – clearly, there are other factors at play. They are explored below.

---

[49]Over the five-year period, CalSTRS, New Jersey, and Pennsylvania PSERS are particularly notable in this regard.

Figure 2.4: **Percentage of ADEC Funded (2013-2017) and Funded Status (2017)**

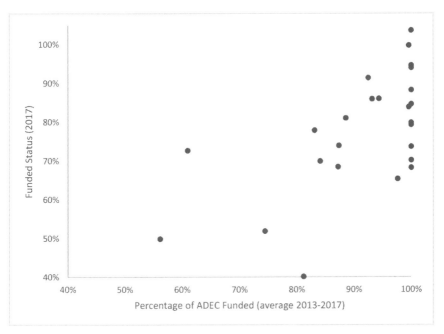

Source: Comprehensive Annual Financial Reports and Public Plans Database, Center for Retirement Research at Boston College. In respect of certain pension systems, 2017 ADEC funding data is not available and for these systems, the average is for the period from 2013 through the end of the available data series. Funded status is based on market value of assets.

Employer contributions to pension systems are generally expressed as a percentage of annual payroll. As a pension system's funded status worsens, required employer contributions become more significant relative to payroll.

Figure 2.5 shows the relationship between ADEC as a percentage of payroll, and funded status. It illustrates that pension systems with weaker funded status (lower on the y-axis) evidence a higher ratio of ADEC to payroll (towards the right on the x-axis).

Figure 2.5: **ADEC as a Percentage of Payroll (2013-2017) and Funded Status (2017)**

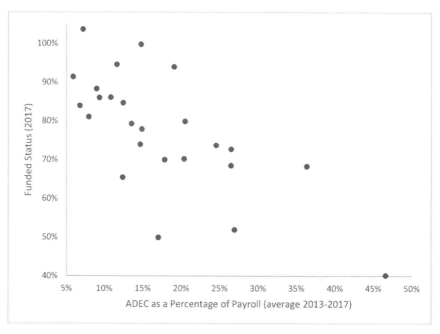

Source: Comprehensive Annual Financial Reports and Public Plans Database, Center for Retirement Research at Boston College. Funded status is based on market value of assets.

2.3 Pension Liabilities and Funded Status

Assets reported by the 25 largest U.S. public pension systems decreased from $1.81 trillion in 2008 to $1.45 trillion in 2009 as a result of the GFC, and then increased to $2.38 trillion in 2017, as shown in Figure 2.6. Over that period, liabilities increased steadily from $2.10 trillion in 2008 to $3.12 trillion in 2017. The combined average funded status of these plans fell from 85% in 2008 to 67% in 2009[50] as plan assets declined by $365 billion while liabilities increased by $95 billion. The average funded status rose to 82% by 2014. The downward trend after that time was slightly ameliorated in 2017 as a result of strong investment gains. The combined funded status of the 25 plans was 77.4% at the end of the study period.

Figure 2.6: **Assets and Liabilities ($ trillion) and Funded Status (2008-2017)**

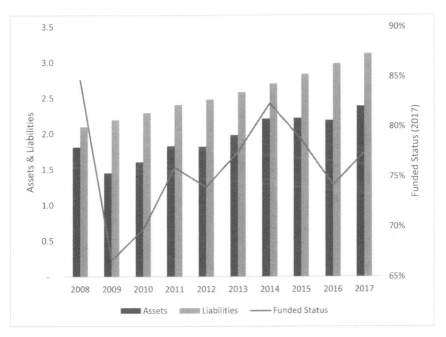

Source: Comprehensive Annual Financial Reports. Assets and funded status are reported at market value.

Figure 2.7 shows that the combined funded status masks a

---

[50]The asset value and funded status calculations reported here are based on market value of assets. Elsewhere in this report, we discuss the actuarial value of assets which is used in some studies to calculate funded status.

wide range between plans, with two (New Jersey and Illinois Teachers) falling below 50%. The Tennessee, Washington State, and Wisconsin pension systems, as well as the two New York State plans, all have funded ratios above 90%.

Figure 2.7: **Funding Gap ($ billion) and Funded Status (2017)**

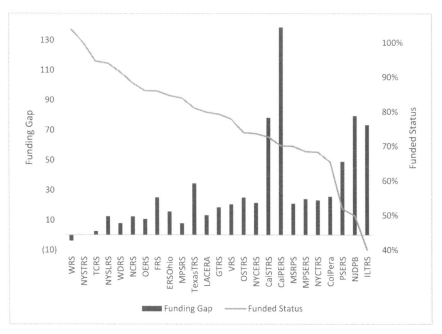

Source: Comprehensive Annual Financial Reports. Funded status and funding gap are based on market value of assets.

Figure 2.8 shows the distribution of pension systems by funded status, with the largest concentration being those with funded status in the 80% to 90% range.

Figure 2.8: **Distribution of 25 Largest Public Pension Systems by Funded Status (2017)**

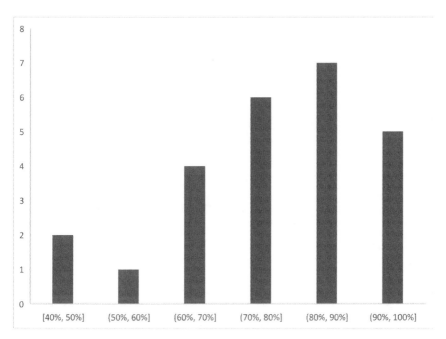

Source: Comprehensive Annual Financial Reports. Column height represents the number of pension systems with funded status in a particular range (for example – there are two pension systems with a funded status of between 40% and 50% and seven pension systems with a funded status between 80% and 90%). Funded status is based on market value of assets.

2.4 Discount Rate

Figure 2.9 shows the discount rate used by each of the 25 plans for 2008 and 2017. As noted, discount rates have decreased as plans have adjusted to lower expected returns (illustrated in more detail in Figure 2.10) and due to constraints introduced by the adoption of GASB 67, as previously noted.

Figure 2.9: **Discount Rate (2008 and 2017)**

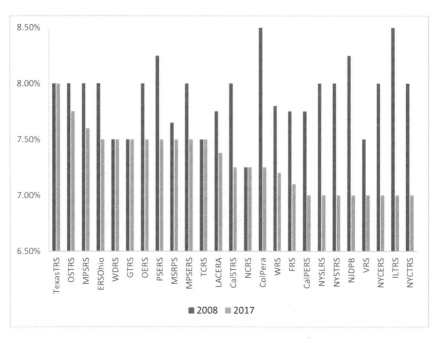

Source: Comprehensive Annual Financial Reports. Certain of the pension systems decreased their discount rates subsequent to the study period.[51]

---

[51]Pension systems that reduced their discount rates subsequent to their 2017 annual reports include CalPERS, which reduced its discount rate to 7.35%, Texas TRS: 7.25%, FRS: 7.5%, ERSOhio: 7.5%, NJDPB: 7.5%, OERS: 7.2%, LACERA: 7.5%, MPSERS: 7.05%, and MPSRS: 7.6%.

Figure 2.10: **Average Discount Rate of 25 Largest Public Pension Systems (2008-2017)**

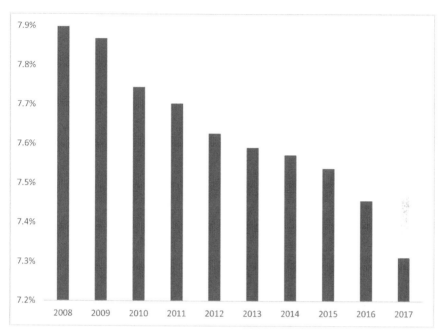

Source: Comprehensive Annual Financial Reports. Data are reported as a simple average of the discount rates.

As shown in Figure 2.11, every one of the pension systems used a discount rate in 2017 (y-axis) that meaningfully exceeds its 10-year trailing investment returns (x-axis). We discuss the relationship between expected returns and the discount rate in more detail below.[52]

---

[52]See in particular, Table 2.3 for further analysis of this relationship.

Figure 2.11: **Discount Rate and Trailing 10-Year Returns (YE 2017)**

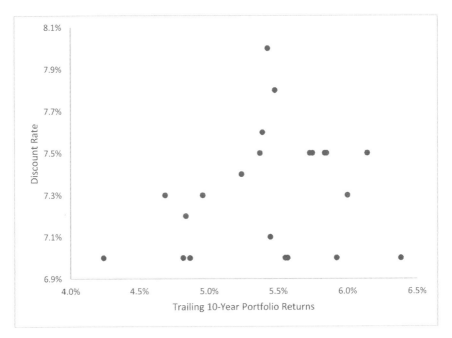

Source: Comprehensive Annual Financial Reports.

The predictive impact of a decrease in the discount rate on pension liabilities is non-linear. A rule of thumb used by actuaries is that a 1% decrease in the discount rate results in an increase in gross pension liabilities of 10-15%.[53] Translated into dollar terms, this means that a 1% decrease in the discount rate across the 25 pension systems in our dataset would result in an increase in liabilities in the range of $312 billion to $468 billion (13-20% of plan assets).

---

[53]See Chen and Matkin (2017).

2.5   Impact of Demographics

Figure 2.12 shows the ratio of active members (those making contributions) to annuitants (those drawing pension benefit payments).[54] This ratio has deteriorated significantly (and surprisingly rapidly) over the decade covered by the data. The number of annuitants for the 25 pension systems increased 36.9% from 4.2 million in 2008 to 5.7 million in 2017[55], while the number of active members declined from 8.3 million to 8.2 million.[56]

Unlike the demography-based argument that U.S. Social Security solvency depends on new workers and their contributions to offset benefits paid to retirees, this issue is actually less of a concern with public pension plans because of the low weight of employee contributions in total pension funding. This was discussed earlier.

---

[54]There is a third category of pension plan members – those who are benefit-eligible, but inactive. This group is not yet receiving pension benefits but is also not presently making contributions into the pension system. Because of inconsistencies in the way that these members are accounted for between pension systems, we have excluded them from the above analysis.

[55]The increase over this period was particularly high for Virginia Retirement System, where the number of annuitants grew 85.3% (107,609 to 199,388). It grew 56% for GTRS (78,633 to 122,629). The increase was lowest for New York State TRS where it was 19.8% (136,706 to 163,818).

[56]The decrease in active members was most acute for Michigan PSERS, where the number of active members decreased 26.8% (278,642 to 203,981), and for New Jersey, where it decreased 16% (522,900 to 328,207). By contrast, New York City TRS, CalPERS, and Colorado PERA experienced growth in active members of 11.0% (109,868 to 122,000), 9.1% (813,474 to 887,220), and 9.0% (190,684 to 207,769), respectively over the period.

Figure 2.12: **Ratio of Active Members to Annuitants (2008-2017)**

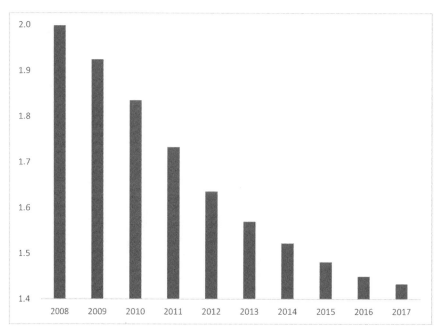

Source: Comprehensive Annual Financial Reports.

Figure 2.13 shows the active-to-annuitant ratio across U.S public pension systems. As expected, the variance between systems is driven to a large extent by inter-regional population movements and general demographic trends. This is illustrated in Figure 2.15, in which states and cities with higher population growth (towards the right of the x-axis) tend to have higher active-to-annuitant ratios (higher on the y-axis).

Figure 2.13: **Ratio of Active Members to Annuitants (2007)**

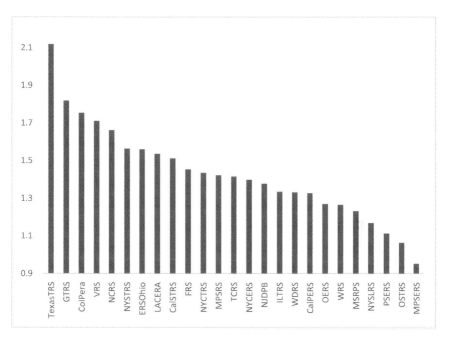

Source: Comprehensive Annual Financial Reports.

Figure 2.14 shows the geographic dispersion of the 25 largest pension plans, with darker shading for states in which a disproportionately large share of the underlying assets is managed.

Figure 2.14: **Geographic Distribution of 25 Largest Public Pension Systems (2017)**

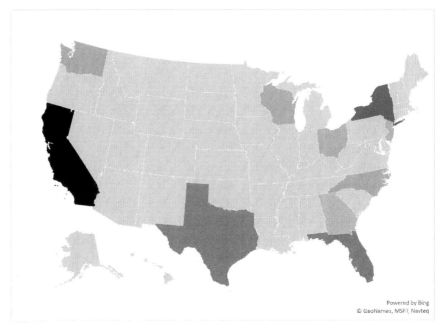

Source: Comprehensive Annual Financial Reports.

Figure 2.15 shows the expected positive relationship between state population growth and the ratio of active members to annuitants.

Figure 2.15: **Population Growth (5 Year) and Ratio of Active Members to Annuitants (2017)**

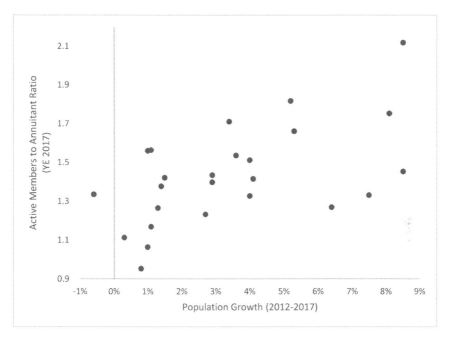

Source: *Comprehensive Annual Financial Reports. State population data from U.S. Census Bureau Population Division, Annual Estimates of the Resident Population for the United States, Regions, States, and Puerto Rico: April 1, 2010 to July 1, 2017 (released December 2017). City population data from Annual Estimates of the Resident Population for Incorporated Places of 50,000 or More, Ranked by July 1, 2017 Population: April 1, 2010 to July 1, 2017 (released May 2018).*

2.6 Benefit Levels

Figure 2.16 shows the pension benefits per annuitant for each of the 25 public pension systems in 2008 and 2017, respectively. The range of per-annuitant benefits is substantial, with teacher retirement systems generally showing higher pension benefits per annuitant.

There appears to be a weak inverse relationship between per-employee benefits and funded status. Plans with the lowest benefit payments per annuitant are associated with higher levels of funding than those with richer benefits. This is also evident in Figure 2.16 – pension systems toward the right of the chart are associated with lower average benefits and higher funding ratios.

Figure 2.16: **Benefits per Annuitant (2008, 2017) and Funded Status (2017)**

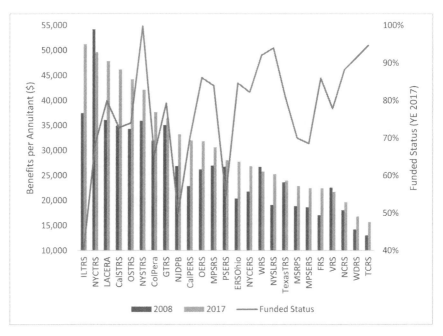

Source: Comprehensive Annual Financial Reports. Benefits per annuitant calculated as total benefit payments in each year divided by number of annuitants. Funded status based on market value of assets.

2.7 Asset Allocation

In many pension portfolios, fixed income and public equity investments have increasingly been displaced by alternative investment strategies (e.g., hedge funds, private equity, real assets). Accounting for 83.7% of portfolios in 2008, traditional asset classes declined to 71.7% of portfolios in 2017, about the same as their percentage in target portfolios (70.2%).[57]

Pension systems began allocating portfolios toward alternative investments in the early 2000s. Hedge fund (absolute return) allocations increased from less than 1% of portfolios in 2008 to 4.8% in 2016. As noted earlier, high fees and poor performance on the part of many hedge funds led several public pension systems to reduce or in some cases eliminate their allocations to this asset class.

Private equity allocations comprised 7.3% of the average public pension portfolio in 2008, and grew to approximately 10.0% in 2011. Since that time private equity allocations have remained slightly below that level.

Real assets, including real estate comprised 6.5% of top-25 pension portfolios in 2007 and 9.1% in 2017. This asset class can be expected to grow within portfolios as this allocation is somewhat short of its 11.9% target.

Some public pension systems have established distinct portfolio allocations for opportunistic investments and for other asset classes, which – although a small portion of total portfolios –

---

[57]Target allocations are expressed as ranges within which an institutional investor seeks to invest its portfolio in particular asset classes. The targets expressed in our analysis represent the mid-point of such ranges as reported by the individual public pension systems.

could expand as asset allocation becomes more sophisticated.

As we have noted, asset allocation is based on three inputs: Expected asset class returns, expected risk (in the form of *ex ante* volatility of expected returns), and correlations between asset classes. Figure 2.17 shows the evolving average asset allocation of the pension systems in our sample between 2008 and 2017.

Figure 2.17: **Average Asset Allocation of 25 Largest Public Pension Systems (2008-2017)**

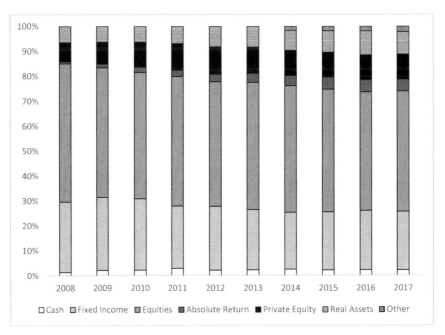

Source: Comprehensive Annual Financial Reports. Chart shows simple average asset allocation based on market value of assets at year end. Real Assets includes Real Estate, which is reported as a distinct asset class by some pension systems.

Pension fund investors generally try to match their assets to their liabilities in terms of magnitude and duration. In practice, perfect asset-liability matching is viable only for pension plans that are close to being fully funded and therefore can build duration-based fixed income portfolios. As noted, most public pension plans need to out-earn the returns they might otherwise achieve with fixed income investments.

The increase in longer-duration exposures associated with alternatives such as private equity is shown in Figure 2.17. Pension systems have adopted these increased allocations because of portfolio benefits that include the expected illiquidity premium on such investments, cash yields generated by some of them – yield is necessary to offset the negative cash flows that are generally uniform among established pension systems, portfolio diversification, and access to incremental sources of market returns.

Pension systems have not uniformly adopted alternative investments. Figure 2.18 illustrates the distribution of allocations to traditional asset classes (fixed income and equities) in 2017 among the plans in our sample. At one extreme, the portfolio of the Teachers Retirement System of Georgia had virtually no exposure to alternative asset classes and the North Carolina Retirement System was moving in that direction.[58] At the other extreme, the Teachers' Retirement System of the State of Illinois allocated 48% of its portfolio to alternative asset classes. Of the largest 25 pension plans, 18 allocated more than 25% of their portfolios to alternative investments in 2017.

---

[58]In April 2017, North Carolina's State Treasurer announced that NCRS would divest from all alternative investments, stating, "It's not emotional. It's not political. It's mathematical....We don't own alternative investments. They own us. I think they increase complexity and reduce value." (https://www.bloomberg.com/news/articles/2017-04-07/the-90-billion-investor-who-s-out-to-fire-wall-street).

Figure 2.18: **Distribution of Target Allocations to Alternative Asset Classes (2017)**

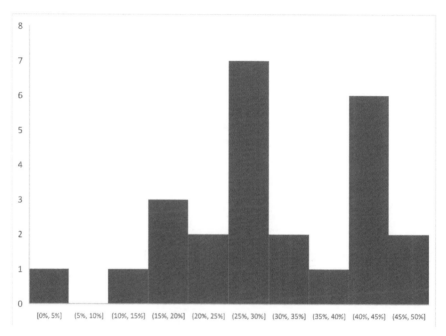

Source: Comprehensive Annual Financial Reports. Column height represents the number of pension systems with an allocation to alternative asset classes in a particular range (for example –there is one pension system with an allocation of between 0% and 5% and there are seven with an allocation of between 25% and 30%).

Figure 2.19 investigates whether there is a correlation between asset allocation and funded status. Have pension systems with weaker funded status increased their exposure to hedge funds and longer-dated private capital strategies in order to capture what they believe may be excess and uncorrelated returns? If so, we would expect to find points plotted parallel to the downward sloping line in this chart, with pension systems that have weaker funded status (towards the left on the x-axis) exhibiting higher allocations to alternative investments (higher on the y-axis) and pension systems that are close to being fully funded (towards the right on the x-axis) exhibiting lower allocations to these asset classes (lower on the y-axis). Visually, this relationship is weakly evident.

Figure 2.19: **Funded Status and Allocation to Alternative Investments (2017)**

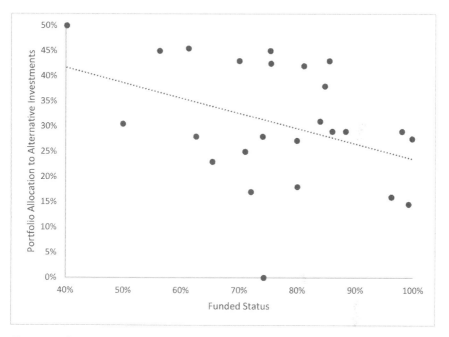

Source: *Comprehensive Annual Financial Reports.*

Most alternative investment strategies (with the exception of hedge funds) require capital to be committed and drawn-down over time, with the result that there is usually a gap between target and actual allocations as these strategies are incorporated into or expanded within portfolios. Likewise, if the portfolio weight of an illiquid asset class is reduced, it can take several years for that decision to become evident in portfolio composition – as proceeds from the realization of investments are gradually redeployed into other asset classes.

This is illustrated in Figure 2.20, which shows, for example, that the actual allocation to real assets in 2017 across the cohort of pension systems was 2.8% lower than the target allocation. Asset classes above the diagonal can be expected to increase as a component of portfolios in future years, while those below the diagonal are likely to decrease in portfolio allocations.

Figure 2.20: **Target and Actual Asset Allocation (2017)**

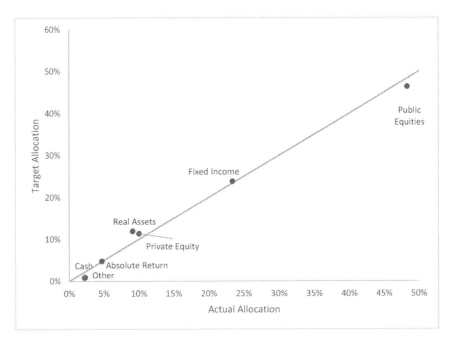

Source: Comprehensive Annual Financial Reports. Chart shows simple average target and actual allocation based on market value of assets, at year end. Real Assets includes Real Assets and Real Estate. Asset classes above the line are those with an actual allocation that is lower than their target allocation, while asset classes below the line are those with an actual allocation that exceeds their target allocation.

2.8 Investment Performance

In light of how pension systems allocate their portfolios, we next evaluate the impact on portfolio performance.

A cursory look at Figure 2.21 suggests that the portfolios with the lowest allocation to alternatives (those towards the left) have generated after-fee returns that are no worse than those of pension plans that have made a much larger allocation to alternatives. This is true for the decade through 2017 (lower line) and for the five-year period ending in 2017 (upper line). All portfolios performed at higher rates of return over the shorter time period.

The observation in Figure 2.21 is surprising, particularly in light of the primacy of asset allocation in portfolio construction. The apparent absence of a relationship between allocation to alternatives and pension fund investment performance does not suggest that alternative investments do not add value. It may have more to do with the strong performance of public equity and bond markets over the decade through 2017, or to the "drag" of high investment expenses, reducing what might be stronger gross returns from alternative investments balanced against much lower fees on traditional investments. Since fees (particularly management fees) are certain, while portfolio returns are not, fees should be assigned a correspondingly high degree of importance in pension fund asset selection. We return to this topic below.

This observation may also be due to the inability of pension fund investors to select the best underlying fund managers on a consistent basis. An exceptional investment office may have superior ability always to select the best managers and funds (all managers have certain underperforming funds). However, extrapolating across the entire public pension system, there is something of a zero-sum game. One pension fund's gain (in a trade or a fund investment) becomes another's loss. This applies to traditional equities and fixed income investments and – as the industry matures – might equally apply to certain alternative investing strategies, particularly those that focus on secondary transactions and not on development of new businesses or assets.

Figure 2.21: **Asset Allocation and Portfolio Investment Returns (2008-2017)**

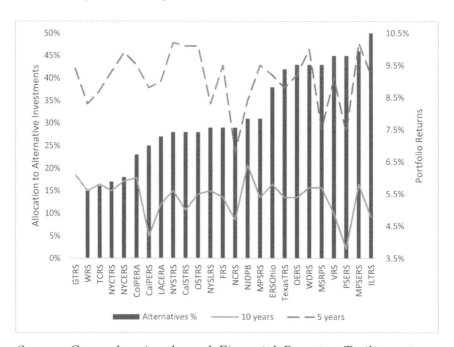

Source: Comprehensive Annual Financial Reports. Trailing returns are calculated using a geometric mean calculation and may differ from annualized returns reported by pension systems which may be time-weighted.[59]

---

[59]Specifically, annualized performance is calculated using the formula: $[\sum_{i=1}^{n}(1+\text{Annual Return}_i)]^{\frac{1}{n}}-1$ with $i = 1, ..., n$ years.

A common approach used by pension systems to determine their expected portfolio return is called the "building block" method. The expected return for each asset class is multiplied by the weight of that asset class in the portfolio. Adding expected inflation to the sum of these products yields an expected nominal portfolio return which – subject to certain constraints introduced by GASB 67 and 68 – is used to guide determination of the discount rate used in determining the present value of pension liabilities.

Figure 2.22 shows the target returns that the 25 plans in our dataset expect to earn in each asset class. There is a surprisingly wide range of returns expected for identical asset classes.[60] The reasons include the weighting of different asset types within each asset class,[61] as well as differing perspectives of the investment staff, trustees, and investment consultants for each pension system.

The inflation estimates used by the 25 largest U.S. pension plans averaged 2.6% and ranged from 2.2% to 3.1%.

Under a "wisdom of crowds" assumption, the average (represented by the circle on the vertical lines) may be an appropriate view of the perspectives of the largest U.S public pension systems for future returns in each asset class and for future inflation.

---

[60]New Jersey has the highest expectations in real terms for four asset classes – fixed income, private equity, real estate, and real assets, Georgia TRS has the highest expectation for public equities and the lowest expectation for fixed income, and Virginia has the lowest expectation for both public equities and real assets.

[61]For example – real estate portfolios range from higher returning opportunistic strategies to lower-risk core strategies and may also include investments in real estate debt as well as public equity investments in REITs.

Figure 2.22: **Range of Expected Long-Term Rate of Return by Asset Class (2017)**

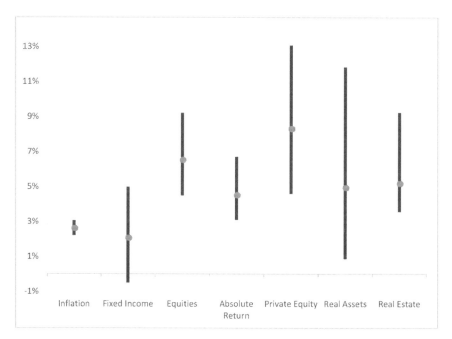

Source: Comprehensive Annual Financial Reports. Vertical lines illustrate range of minimum to maximum expected performance by pension system. Circle represents average for each asset class.

Figure 2.23 shows the actual trailing 5-year investment performance by asset class as well as the simple average for each asset class held by the 25 pension systems. We observe a wide spread in performance within each asset class, illustrating the importance of portfolio composition and exposure selection and execution.

Figure 2.23: **Range of Investment Performance by Asset Class (Trailing 5-years, 2017)**

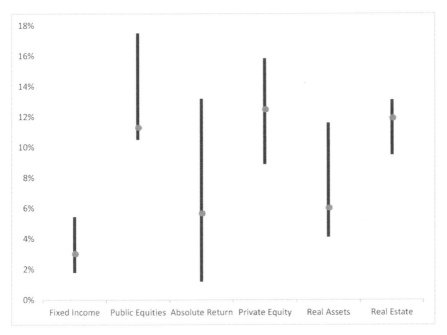

Source: Comprehensive Annual Financial Reports. Column height represents the number of pension systems with an allocation to alternative asset classes in a particular range (for example – there is one pension system with an allocation of between 0% and 5% and there are seven with an allocation of between 25% and 30%).

Figure 2.24 plots expected returns against trailing 5-year returns for each asset class. Data points above the diagonal represent asset classes for which the 25 pension plans expect to earn above what they achieved over the previous five years, while data points below the diagonal indicate expectations that are below prior performance.

Figure 2.24: **Expected Returns (2017) and Historical Returns by Asset Class (Trailing 5-Years)**

Source: Comprehensive Annual Financial Reports. Data presented is simple average for 25 largest pension systems. Expected nominal returns are as reported in 2017 annual reports and incorporate the average expected inflation assumption for the sample, which is 2.6%. This chart excludes Commodities, which has trailing 5-year returns of negative 6.0% and expected nominal returns of 5.5% as well as certain asset classes that are reported by too few pension systems to be statistically significant.

In Table 2.2 we present the annual net return achieved by each pension system for the years 2008-2017. In Table 2.3 we show the trailing 3-year, 5-year, and 10- year performance and expected real and nominal rates of return, as well as the discount rate for the plans (recall that expected returns determine the discount rate). Table 2.3 (as with Figure 2.11) suggests that most pension systems use a discount rate (column 7) that, while below trailing 5-year returns (column 2), is above trailing 10-year returns (column 3).

Table 2.2: Annual Portfolio Performance (2008-2017)

2008	2009	2010	2011	2012	2013	2014	2015	2016	2017
NYSLRS 2.6%	WRS 21.8%	NYSLRS 25.9%	ILTRS 23.6%	ERSOhio 14.5%	ColPera 15.6%	CalSTRS 18.3%	NYSLRS 7.0%	MSRPS 10.0%	ColPera 18.1%
WDRS 1.2%	ERSOhio 19.1%	MSRPS 20.0%	NYCTRS 23.3%	MPSERS 13.5%	NJDPB 14.4%	NYSTRS 18.2%	OSTRS 5.4%	ERSOhio 8.3%	ERSOhio 16.8%
TCRS -1.2%	ColPera 17.4%	OERS 17.0%	NYSTRS 23.2%	MSRPS 13.4%	MSRPS 14.4%	CalPERS 17.7%	NYSTRS 5.2%	WRS 8.3%	NYCERS 16.8%
LACERA -1.5%	MSRPS 14.0%	TexasTRS 15.7%	NYCERS 23.1%	NJDPB 13.1%	ERSOhio 14.4%	NYCTRS 17.6%	WDRS 4.9%	MPSERS 7.6%	WRS 16.2%
TexasTRS -2.1%	MPSERS -6.1%	PSERS 14.6%	CalSTRS 22.8%	ColPera 12.9%	NYSTRS 13.7%	FRS 17.4%	VRS 4.7%	ColPera 7.3%	OSTRS 14.3%
NCRS -2.1%	GTRS -13.1%	NYCTRS 14.4%	OSTRS 22.6%	MSRPS 10.6%	OSTRS 13.7%	ILTRS 17.4%	CalSTRS 4.5%	NJDPB 7.0%	MPSERS 13.8%
NJDPB -2.7%	NCRS -14.2%	VRS 14.1%	OERS 22.3%	NYSLRS 6.0%	CalSTRS 13.6%	GTRS 17.2%	MPSRS 4.5%	TCRS 2.8%	FRS 13.6%
PSERS -2.8%	TCRS -15.3%	NYCERS 14.1%	TexasTRS 22.2%	TCRS 5.6%	GTRS 13.3%	WDRS 17.1%	OERS 4.3%	WDRS 2.7%	CalSTRS 13.4%
GTRS -3.4%	NJDPB -15.5%	FRS 14.0%	FRS 22.1%	PSERS 3.4%	CalPERS 13.2%	NYCERS 17.0%	TexasTRS 4.2%	NYSTRS 2.3%	WDRS 13.4%
OERS -3.8%	NYCTRS -18.1%	ColPera 14.0%	CalPERS 22.1%	NYSTRS 2.8%	WRS 13.2%	MPSRS 16.9%	LACERA 4.1%	VRS 1.9%	NJDPB 13.1%
CalSTRS -4.0%	LACERA -18.2%	ERSOhio 14.0%	MPSRS 21.7%	TexasTRS 2.7%	FRS 13.1%	OSTRS 16.8%	ILTRS 4.0%	NYCTRS 1.9%	TexasTRS 12.9%
VRS -4.4%	MPSRS -18.9%	OSTRS 13.5%	GTRS 21.4%	OSTRS 2.3%	ILTRS 12.8%	OERS 16.6%	GTRS 3.7%	MPSRS 1.8%	NYCTRS 12.9%
FRS -4.4%	FRS -19.0%	NJDPB 13.4%	WDRS 21.3%	NCRS 2.2%	OERS 12.7%	LACERA 16.5%	FRS 3.7%	NYCERS 1.5%	LACERA 12.7%
MPSRS -4.6%	NYSTRS -20.5%	CalPERS 13.3%	PSERS 21.1%	GTRS 2.2%	MPSERS 12.5%	TCRS 16.5%	TCRS 3.3%	GTRS 1.4%	GTRS 12.5%
NYCERS -5.0%	VRS -21.1%	WDRS 13.2%	LACERA 20.4%	NYCTRS 1.9%	WDRS 12.4%	NCRS 15.9%	NYCERS 3.1%	CalSTRS 1.4%	ILTRS 12.5%
ILTRS -5.0%	OSTRS -21.7%	ILTRS 12.9%	TCRS 20.2%	OERS 1.6%	MPSRS 12.3%	VRS 15.7%	PSERS 3.0%	TexasTRS 1.3%	MPSRS 12.5%
CalPERS -5.1%	TexasTRS -21.9%	MPSRS 12.9%	VRS 19.6%	MPSRS 1.6%	NYCERS 12.2%	MPSERS 15.6%	NYCTRS 3.0%	PSERS 1.3%	NYSTRS 12.5%
OSTRS -5.4%	OERS -22.3%	NYSTRS 12.7%	NCRS 19.1%	WDRS 1.6%	LACERA 11.9%	PSERS 14.9%	NCRS 2.3%	OERS 1.2%	VRS 12.1%
NYCTRS -6.2%	ILTRS -22.7%	NCRS 12.1%	CalSTRS 18.5%	NYCERS 1.4%	NYCTRS 11.9%	MPSERS 13.0%	CalPERS 2.2%	OSTRS 0.9%	OERS 11.9%
NYSTRS -6.4%	WDRS -22.8%	CalSTRS 12.0%	WDRS 17.8%	ILTRS 1.3%	VRS 11.8%	NJDPB 10.4%	MPSERS 2.1%	LACERA 0.8%	TCRS 11.4%
MPSERS -12.3%	CalPERS -24.0%	WRS 12.0%	MPSERS 14.6%	FRS 0.8%	NYSLRS 10.4%	ERSOhio 7.3%	ColPera 1.5%	NCRS 0.8%	NYSLRS 11.4%
MSRPS -20.0%	CalSTRS -25.1%	LACERA 11.6%	ColPera 6.6%	CalPERS 0.3%	TexasTRS 10.2%	TCRS 7.0%	MSRPS 1.2%	FRS 0.5%	CalPERS 11.2%
ColPera -26.0%	NYSLRS -26.4%	GTRS 11.1%	WRS 1.9%	LACERA 0.1%	TCRS 9.9%	WRS 5.7%	NJDPB 0.6%	CalPERS 0.5%	PSERS 10.1%
WRS -26.3%	PSERS -26.5%	TCRS 10.2%	MSRPS 1.3%	LACERA 0.1%	NCRS 9.5%	WRS 5.4%	ERSOhio 0.3%	NYSLRS 0.0%	MSRPS 10.0%
ERSOhio -27.2%		MPSERS 8.8%	ERSOhio 0.4%		PSERS 8.0%	MSRPS 2.7%	WRS -0.6%	ILTRS 0.0%	NCRS 6.0%

Source: Comprehensive Annual Financial Reports.

Table 2.3: Trailing Portfolio Performance (3, 5, and 10-years) as at YE 2017

3-years		5-years		10-years		Expected (real)		Expected Inflation		Expected (nominal)		Discount Rate	
ColPera	8.8%	NYSTRS	10.2%	NJDPB	6.4%	NJDPB	7.7%	NJDPB	2.5%	NJDPB	10.2%	NJDPB	7.0%
ERSOhio	8.3%	MPSERS	10.2%	GTRS	6.1%	FRS	6.9%	FRS	2.6%	FRS	9.5%	FRS	7.1%
MPSERS	7.7%	OSTRS	10.1%	ColPera	6.0%	ILTRS	6.8%	ILTRS	2.5%	ILTRS	9.3%	ILTRS	7.0%
WRS	7.7%	CalSTRS	10.1%	NYCERS	5.9%	GTRS	6.3%	GTRS	2.8%	GTRS	9.1%	GTRS	7.5%
MSRPS	7.0%	WDRS	10.0%	ERSOhio	5.8%	WDRS	5.9%	WDRS	3.0%	WDRS	8.9%	WDRS	7.5%
NYCERS	6.9%	NYCERS	9.9%	TCRS	5.8%	OERS	6.3%	OERS	2.5%	OERS	8.8%	OERS	7.5%
WDRS	6.9%	FRS	9.5%	MPSERS	5.8%	OSTRS	6.3%	OSTRS	2.5%	OSTRS	8.8%	OSTRS	7.5%
NJDPB	6.8%	ColPera	9.5%	MSRPS	5.7%	CalSTRS	5.4%	CalSTRS	2.8%	CalSTRS	8.2%	CalSTRS	7.3%
OSTRS	6.7%	MPSRS	9.5%	WDRS	5.7%	ERSOhio	5.7%	ERSOhio	2.5%	ERSOhio	8.2%	ERSOhio	7.5%
NYSTRS	6.6%	GTRS	9.4%	WRS	5.6%	MPSERS	5.5%	MPSERS	2.3%	MPSERS	7.8%	MPSERS	7.5%
CalSTRS	6.3%	NYCTRS	9.3%	NYCTRS	5.6%	NYSTRS	5.1%	NYSTRS	2.5%	NYSTRS	7.6%	NYSTRS	7.3%
MPSRS	6.2%	ERSOhio	9.2%	NYSTRS	5.6%	NYCTRS	5.1%	NYCTRS	2.5%	NYCTRS	7.6%	NYCTRS	7.0%
VRS	6.1%	OERS	9.2%	OSTRS	5.6%	TCRS	4.5%	TCRS	3.0%	TCRS	7.5%	TCRS	7.5%
NYSLRS	6.0%	ILTRS	9.2%	FRS	5.5%	NCRS	4.3%	NCRS	3.1%	NCRS	7.4%	NCRS	7.2%
TexasTRS	6.0%	VRS	9.1%	TexasTRS	5.4%	LACERA	4.6%	LACERA	2.8%	LACERA	7.4%	LACERA	7.4%
NYCTRS	5.8%	LACERA	9.0%	MPSRS	5.4%	NYSLRS	4.6%	NYSLRS	2.8%	NYSLRS	7.3%	NYSLRS	7.0%
FRS	5.8%	TexasTRS	8.8%	OERS	5.4%	VRS	4.8%	VRS	2.5%	VRS	7.3%	VRS	7.0%
GTRS	5.8%	CalPERS	8.8%	LACERA	5.2%	PSERS	4.4%	PSERS	2.8%	PSERS	7.2%	PSERS	7.3%
TCRS	5.8%	TCRS	8.7%	CalSTRS	5.0%	MSRPS	4.4%	MSRPS	2.7%	MSRPS	7.1%	MSRPS	7.5%
LACERA	5.7%	NJDPB	8.4%	VRS	4.9%	NYCERS	4.5%	NYCERS	2.5%	NYCERS	7.0%	NYCERS	7.0%
OERS	5.7%	WRS	8.3%	ILTRS	4.8%	WRS	4.2%	WRS	2.8%	WRS	7.0%	WRS	7.2%
ILTRS	5.4%	NYSLRS	8.3%	NCRS	4.7%	MPSRS	4.6%	MPSRS	2.3%	MPSRS	6.9%	MPSRS	7.8%
PSERS	4.8%	MSRPS	7.5%	CalPERS	4.2%	TexasTRS	4.6%	TexasTRS	2.2%	TexasTRS	6.8%	TexasTRS	8.0%
CalPERS	4.5%	PSERS	7.4%	PSERS	3.8%	ColPera	4.2%	ColPera	2.4%	ColPera	6.6%	ColPera	7.3%
NCRS	3.0%	NCRS	6.8%			CalPERS	3.4%	CalPERS	2.5%	CalPERS	5.9%	CalPERS	7.2%

Source: *Comprehensive Annual Financial Reports.*

2.9 Investment Expenses

Reporting of investment expenses by U.S. pension systems is incomplete. Figure 2.25 shows the aggregate reported expenses and the expense ratio by year for the 25 largest pension systems. The increase in the expense ratio of the pension systems over the time period covered in this chart is likely explained by the increasing adoption of more expensive alternative investment strategies.

Figure 2.25: **Aggregate Reported Investment Expenses ($ billion, 2011 - 2017)**

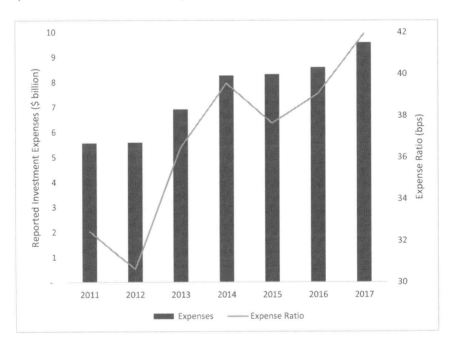

Source: Comprehensive Annual Financial Reports. Expense ratio calculated as total investment expenses divided by average assets at market value.

In most cases, pension systems report management fees in their annual reports, but not consistently or comparably. Expense reporting excludes performance fees and carried interest, which are particularly relevant in the case of alternative invest-ment strategies (a small number of pension systems report these expenses in subsidiary schedules, although this disclosure is in-consistent).

Internal investment expenses – the cost of maintaining invest-ment teams – likewise are not reported in plan annual reports. These expenses are referenced by a small minority of plans in their annual budgets, which are made public. Because of lim-itations in disclosure, it is not possible to determine the total expense ratio associated with management of pension plan port-folios.[62] Because much of the disclosure limitations apply to al-ternative investment strategies, it is likely that the pension sys-tem that comes closest to reporting total investment expenses is Georgia TRS. As noted earlier, that system's portfolio is allo-cated to traditional asset classes for which fees are fully disclosed.

Figure 2.26 shows reported expenses and the expense ratio in 2017 for each pension system.

---

[62]Investment performance and plan assets are reported net of fees such that the non-disclosure of expenses is only relevant to calculations of the gross-net spread on investment returns.

Figure 2.26: **Reported Investment Expenses ($ million) and Expense Ratio (2017)**

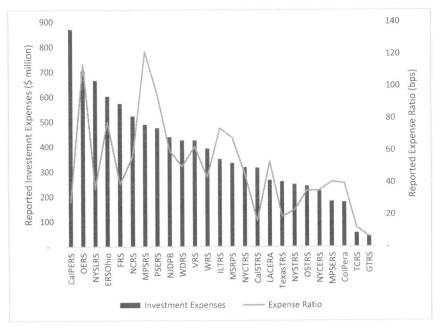

Source: Comprehensive Annual Financial Reports. Expense ratio calculated as total investment expenses divided by average assets at market value.

To illustrate challenges in drawing inferences from the way in which expenses are reported in annual reports, we highlight four cases – CalSTRS, New York State and Local Retirement System, Texas TRS, and Pennsylvania PSERS.

The left three columns in Table 2.4 illustrate investment expenses as reported by CalSTRS in its 2017 annual report. A footnote to this disclosure introduces a significant caveat, "Investment expenses reflected in this table generally represent direct costs associated with investing. Certain expenses including carried interest and management fees related to private assets are not included; however, they are reflected within the net asset value." This means that disclosure does not – in the case of alternative investment strategies – include any fees paid to third-party investment firms that manage CalSTRS' assets, rather those fees are embedded in portfolio values.

The Investment Committee of CalSTRS' Board of Trustees requested in November 2016 that investment staff provide transparency on all investment expenses. A consultant was retained to collate the data, some of which had to be obtained directly from investment managers to which CalSTRS had allocated capital. On January 30, 2019, CalSTRS staff presented to the Investment Committee an Annual Investment Cost Report for 2017. The right eight columns of Table 2.4 are CalSTRS' expenses as disclosed in this report. The report provides schedules for expenses incurred in respect of both externally-managed assets and internally-managed assets.

The annual report and cost report data are not directly comparable as the former is for the fiscal year ending June 30, 2017 and the latter is for the calendar year ending December 31, 2017. Expense ratios are nevertheless comparable. Whereas the annual report shows an expense ratio of 11.0 bps (column three), the cost report shows that the true expense ratio is more than 4.5 times that, at 50.6 bps (column ten), and inclusive of carried interest is 84.0bps, 7.6 times the amount reported (column eleven).

Table 2.4: CalSTRS Investment Expenses ($ million or bps, 2017)

| | Annual Report | | | Investment Cost Report | | | | | | | |
| | | | | Externally Managed | | Internally Managed | | Aggregate | | | |
	NAV	Expenses	Expense Ratio bps	NAV	Expenses	NAV	Expenses	NAV	Expenses	Expense Ratio bps	Incl Carried Interest bps
Global Equity	117,746	167	14.2	60,247	154	58,563	16	118,810	170	14.3	14.4
Corporate Governance	-	-	N/A	4,338	62	1,364	1	5,702	63	110.5	134.2
Fixed Income	30,725	20	6.6	4,852	14	25,097	9	29,949	23	7.7	7.6
Private Equity	16,911	8	4.5	17,114	364	-	N/A	17,114	364	212.7	521.0
Real Estate	26,230	16	5.9	25,993	348	-	N/A	25,993	348	133.9	201.5
Inflation Sensitive	2,759	1	2.6	2,614	39	679	0	3,293	39	118.4	127.8
Risk Mitigating Strategies	10,657	8	7.1	7,299	79	5,021	2	12,320	81	65.7	71.7
Innovative Strategies	413	0	2.6	443	6	-	N/A	443	6	135.4	131.5
Strategic Overlay	200	9	NR	13	9	431	1	444	10		
Cash/liquidity	3,058	1	2.6	-	-	4,149	1	4,149	1	2.4	
	208,700	229	11.0	122,913	1,075	95,304	30	218,217	1,105	50.6	84.0

Source: CalSTRS Comprehensive Annual Financial Report 2017 (fiscal year ending June 30, 2017) and Annual Investment Cost Report to CalSTRS Investment Committee (data for year ending December 31, 2017), presented on January 30, 2019. A summary table in the Annual Investment Cost Report shows external expenses exclusive of carried interest (column five) and internal expenses (column seven). Subsidiary schedules for each asset class show expense ratios (but not dollar expenses) inclusive of carried interest (column eleven). Other discrepancies between columns ten and eleven are due to rounding or different reporting methodologies within the CalSTRS report. Total expenses inclusive of carried interest are approximately $1.8 billion. Expenses associated with the Innovative Strategies portfolio were below $1 million in CalSTRS' annual report.

We turn now to a second example of expense reporting – New York State and Local Retirement System. In the primary expense disclosure in its 2017 annual report (left three columns of Table 2.5), NYSLRS does not report carried interest on private equity investments. An auxiliary schedule (Table 2.6) reports this line item. The right two columns in Table 2.5 include total private equity expenses as well as capitalized expenses for real estate investments that are also disclosed separately in the annual report. The total impact of this disclosure is that while the primary report shows an expense ratio of 33.2 bps, the additional disclosure illustrates that the actual ratio (excluding internal expenses and $21 million in trading commissions) is 50.4 bps.

Table 2.5: **NYSLRS Investment Expenses ($ million or bps, 2017)**

	Annual Report			Estimated Total Expenses	
	NAV	*Expenses*	*Expense Ratio bps*	*Expenses*	*Expense Ratio bps*
Domestic Equity	69,851.7	48.9	7.0	48.9	7.0
International Equity	33,836.7	95.6	28.3	95.6	28.3
Fixed Income	44,802.9	12.0	2.7	12.0	2.7
Private Equity	15,348.5	185.7	121.0	490.2	319.4
Real Estate	12,937.5	61.6	47.6	80.9	47.6
Real Assets	390.6	12.2	312.1	12.2	312.1
Absolute Return Strategy Funds	7,523.8	193.7	257.5	193.7	257.5
Opportunistic Funds	2,065.7	28.4	137.3	36.1	137.3
Short-term Investments	5,653.3				
	192,410.6	638.2	33.2	969.7	50.4

Source: Comprehensive Annual Financial Report 2017.

Table 2.6: **NYSLRS Private Equity Expense Ratio (in bps, 2017)**

Management Fees (expensed)	185.7
Management Fees (capitalized)	26.1
Partnership Expenses	81.2
Carried Interest	197.3
Total Expenses	490.2
Expense Ratio	319.4

Source: Comprehensive Annual Financial Report 2017.

A third illustration is that of Texas TRS. Its 2017 annual report (dated August 31, 2017) includes an auxiliary schedule of administrative and investment expenses for the year ended June 30, 2017, which reports total investment fees of $1.27 billion, suggesting an expense ratio of 89.5 bps. This excludes $53.5 million in brokerage commissions and internal investment expenses. Reacting to the expense burden, the Texas TRS Chief Investment Officer proposed adding 120 new staff in order to bring more of the system's investment activity in-house, which he noted could reduce fees by "at least $600 million."[63]

---

[63]https://www.bloomberg.com/news/articles/2018-03-23/texas-teachers-pension-eyes-hiring-spree-for-investment-group.

Table 2.7: **Texas TRS Investment Expenses ($ million or bps, 2017)**

	NAV	Mgmt Fees (Expensed)	Perf Fees (Expensed)	Mgmt Fees (Netted)	Perf. Fees, Carried Interest (Netted)	Total Expenses	Expense Ratio
U.S. Equities	26,086	30.6	8.6	10.9	7.9	57.9	22.2
Developed Market Equities	22,128	15.7	20.4	16.9	5.7	58.6	26.5
Emerging Market Equities	13,951	32.5	11.1	5.4	1.1	50.1	35.9
Directional Hedge Funds	5,803	2.2	0.5	68.2	52.4	123.4	212.6
Private Equity	17,832			171.9	271.6	443.5	248.7
U.S. Treasuries	10,828						
Absolute Return	3,971			6.6	3.7	10.4	26.1
Stable Value Hedge Funds	5,491			93.7	68.9	162.6	296.2
Global Inflation Linked Bonds	5,047						
Real Assets	17,156	0.6		158.3	109.1	268	156.2
ENRI	5,565	0.6	0.1	60	22	82.8	148.7
Commodities	104						
Risk Parity	6,997	1.6	11.4	1.2	14.2	20.3	
Cash	1,079						
	142,039	83.8	40.6	603.3	543.6	1,271.40	89.5

Source: Report on Investment Activities within Comprehensive Annual Financial Report 2017.

Our final exhibit on investment expenses focuses on Pennsylvania PSERS. As discussed elsewhere, Pennsylvania has become a battleground over investment expenses. An extensive report commissioned by the State Treasurer evaluated the investment expenses of Pennsylvania's two large public pension systems, Pennsylvania Public School Employees' Retirement System (PSERS) and Pennsylvania State Employees' Retirement System (SERS).[64] Investment expenses reported by PSERS in its 2017 annual report reflect an expense ratio of 80.6 bps (left five columns of Table 2.8), however this excludes performance fees and carried interest on certain fixed income funds as well as performance fees and carried interest on real estate and alternative investment funds. The Commission's report estimated these additional expenses at $577 million (column six) suggesting a total expense ratio (excluding internal expenses) of 182.8 bps (column eight).

---

[64]https://www.patreasury.gov/pdf/2018-PPMAIRC-FINAL.pdf.

Table 2.8: **Pennsylvania PSERS Investment Expenses (\$ million or bps, 2017)**

| | Annual Report | | | | Commission Report | | | |
	NAV	Base Expenses	Perf Fees	Total	Expenses Ratio	Estimated	Total Expenses	Expense Ratio
Domestic Equity	6,910.1	1.5	1.5	3.0	4.3	-	3.0	4.3
International Equity	4,243.0	19.8	5.4	25.2	59.4	-	25.2	59.4
Fixed Income	18,660.5	87.5	21.0	108.5	58.1	81.0	189.5	101.6
Real Estate	6,146.7	50.6	-	50.6	82.3	160.0	210.6	342.6
Alternative Investments	7,910.0	102.7	-	102.7	129.8	336.0	438.7	554.6
Absolute Return	5,082.0	78.2	50.7	128.9	253.6	-	128.9	253.6
Commodities	4,052.4	4.1		4.1	10.1	-	4.1	10.1
MLPs	2,369.6	8.3	0.2	8.5	35.9	-	8.5	35.9
Risk Parity	1,055.0	19.6	3.5	23.1	219.0	-	23.1	219.0
	56,429.3	372.3	82.3	454.6	80.6	577.0	1,031.6	182.8

Source: Comprehensive Annual Financial Report 2017 and Public Pension Management and Asset Investment Review Commission: Final Report and Recommendations.

Our intent in providing examples of expense reporting for four of the largest public pension systems is to illustrate the complexity and limitations in determining expense ratios based exclusively on disclosures in annual reports.

The 25 pension systems in our dataset disclose investment expenses of \$9.6 billion in their 2017 annual reports, an expense ratio of 42 bps based on average assets at market value. We have suggested that this significantly underestimates the total expense burden of managing the portfolios of these pension systems.

Assuming an average expense ratio of 80 bps[65] for the 25 pen-

---

[65]We select this average based on peer group data in CalSTRS' cost report. In that report, CalSTRS compares its own calculated expense ratio with that of a peer group calculated by a third-party benchmark firm. The peer group average of 63.8 bps for 2017 excludes transaction costs and carried interest. Applying a simplified adjustment based on a similar ratio of CalSTRS' total expense ratio (50.6 bps) to its expenses excluding carried interest (38.4 bps) suggests an expense ratio for the group of 84bps which we round to 80bps. https://resources.calstrs.com/publicdocs/Page/

sion systems suggests total investment-related expenses of $18.3 billion. This is 10.9% of the $167.1 billion of pension benefits paid by the 25 pension systems in 2017.[66] Absent adequate disclosure, we are well aware that our estimate may be materially inaccurate and present it for illustrative purposes only. Moreover, we stress that the total expense ratio fluctuates significantly based on investment performance due to the performance related expense component.

Net investment performance – not gross performance – is what ultimately matters. Nevertheless, the gross-net spread and opacity around expense reporting are a matter of increasing focus and raise questions about the efficiency of portfolio management.

As noted, expenses are important. They embody a high degree of negative certainty compared to the positive uncertainty of investment returns, and this "drag" directly reduces the revenue available to fund pension benefits.

CommonPage.aspx?PageName=DocumentDownload&Id=74134417-1b50-4511-a5b7-a46942c4c61e.

[66]Certainly performance-based investment expenses fluctuate meaningfully year-to- year, so this example is intended to be purely illustrative.

3
Infrastructure in the Portfolios of Public Pension Systems

The search for predicable longer-duration cash flows with some degree of inflation protection to meet future pension obligations has led public pension systems to increase their allocations to real assets in general and to infrastructure investments more specifically.

Here we provide a discussion of investments in infrastructure by the 25 largest U.S. public pension systems. We examine the reasons pension systems have included the infrastructure asset class in their portfolios, how they have invested in that asset class, the size of their allocations, the types of exposures they have taken, the degree to which the stated investment objectives have been achieved, and how these investments have performed.

None of the 25 largest U.S. public pension systems has a dedicated asset class component to report its infrastructure allocations. Rather, infrastructure is included within other asset categories and is bounded by an allocation range within those categories.

Among the 25 largest pension plans, 23 have invested in infrastructure or have announced their intent to do so. Among the

21 public pension systems that have actually made infrastructure investments, 15 include infrastructure within their "Real Assets" portfolio segment.[67] Figure 2.17 earlier in this study shows that the Real Assets category grew from 6.5% of the average portfolio in 2008 to 9.1% in 2017. Figure 2.20 shows that this asset category is likely to continue to grow – it is the category with the largest gap between actual and target allocations (the average target being 11.9%).

Two of the top-25 public pension systems report infrastructure within an "Inflation Sensitive" portfolio class,[68] and the rest locate it within the "Private Equity"[69] or "Alternatives"[70] categories.

Why is the portfolio category within which infrastructure is embedded important? It informs the return-stream that the pension fund administrator seeks from infrastructure investments and the benchmark against which it measures performance of the asset class.[71]

In the absence of a viable benchmark to track the performance of private market infrastructure investments, some institutional investors have used "listed infrastructure" benchmarks as a proxy. But listed infrastructure performs very differently from private market infrastructure and this could lead to unintended

---

[67]Two of these pension systems (Texas TRS and Michigan PSERS) use a different name for what is effectively a real asset allocation.

[68]CalSTRS and North Carolina Retirement Systems.

[69]NYSTRS, Ohio PERS, and Tennessee Consolidated Retirement System.

[70]Ohio State Teachers, Oregon ERS, and Colorado PERS.

[71]Expectations from an investment within an inflation-oriented asset class are different from those within a private equity asset class.

underperformance. The CIO of one pension system reported to the investment committee that "the recent underperformance in Real Assets was driven largely by benchmark mismatch in natural resources and infrastructure, where public market indices are used to calibrate private market strategies."[72]

The most common benchmark for infrastructure programs of the 25 largest U.S. public pension systems is $CPI + 4\%$. One pension system among those included in our sample referenced a private market infrastructure index as a benchmark.[73] We return to the importance of benchmarks below.

Infrastructure allocations remain relatively small among the pension systems in our dataset, with an average allocation (based on market value of assets) of 0.68% for the 25 plans – 0.94% including only those plans with active infrastructure programs. The average target allocation for those pension systems reporting such a target (13 of the 25 pension plans) is 2.29%.

---

[72]CIO of Maryland SRPS reporting to the investment committee. Minutes of open meeting of November 21, 2017.

[73]NYSTRS uses a benchmark of the Cambridge Infrastructure Index +20% of U.S. CPI.

Table 3.1: **Infrastructure Allocations (2018)**

	Portfolio Bucket	Actual Allocation	First Reported Commitment	Reported Commitments
California Public Employees Retirement System	Real Assets	1.18%	2003	17
California State Teachers Retirement System	Inflation Sensitive	1.23%	1999	26
Colorado Public Employees Retirement Association	Alternatives	NR	2005	4
Florida Retirement System	Real Assets	0.35%	2004	10
Georgia Teachers Retirement System	N/A	N/A	N/A	-
Illinois Teachers Retirement System	Real Assets	0.92%	2006	6
Los Angeles County Employees Retirement Association	Real Assets	NR	NR	-
Maryland State Retirement and Pension System	Real Assets	1.54%	2008	5
Michigan Public School Employees Retirement System	RE and Infra	1.20%	2008	5
Missouri Public Schools Retirement System	Real Assets	0.34%	2006	5
New Jersey Division of Pension and Benefits	Real Assets	0.18%	2005	1
New York City Employees Retirement System	Real Assets	0.67%	2004	13
New York City Teachers Retirement System	Real Assets	0.91%	2003	18
New York State and Local Retirement System	Real Assets	0.30%	2006	8
New York State Teachers Retirement System	Private Equity	NR	2009	5
North Carolina Retirement Systems	Inflation Sensitive	NR	2004	8
Ohio Public Employees Retirement System	Private Equity	0.36%	2009	5
Ohio State Teachers Retirement System	Alternatives	0.14%	2006	9
Oregon Employees Retirement System	Alternatives	1.00%	2008	17
Pennsylvania Public School Employees Retirement System	Real Assets	2.05%	2007	8
Teacher Retirement System of Texas	ENRI	1.70%	2007	22
Tennessee Consolidated Retirement System	Private Equity	NR	NR	-
Virginia Retirement System	Real Assets	0.82%	1995	19
Washington Department of Retirement Systems	Real Assets	2.05%	2005	16
Wisconsin Retirement System	N/A	N/A	N/A	-

Source: Preqin, Inframation, Comprehensive Annual Financial Reports. The first reported commitment may precede the year in which a formal allocation for infrastructure investing was established by each pension system.

Pension systems publicly articulate their investment strategy – including the reason for the inclusion of a particular type of investment – in their investment policy statements. Table 3.2 summarizes the desired objectives associated with infrastructure allocations. The primary goals are inflation protection, diversification, and current cash flow (yield).

Table 3.2: Objectives of the 25 Largest Public Pension Plans for Investing in Infrastructure

Inflation protection	8
Yield / steady cash flows	8
Diversification	6
Defensive characteristics	3
Capital preservation	2
Long term investment	2
Risk-adjusted returns	2
Upside (capital appreciation, operational enhancement)	2
Steward of infrastructure	1

Source: Investment Policy Statements, Preqin. Number reflects the count of pension systems that articulate each attribute of infrastructure investing as a motive for inclusion of the asset class in their portfolios. Most investment policy statements cite numerous reasons.

Almost all infrastructure investing by U.S. pension systems is through private investment funds. With very limited exceptions,[74] the pension systems themselves have undertaken no direct investing in infrastructure assets. Moreover, almost all commitments have been to finite-life funds[75] with durations of 10-15 years and as much as 25 years in some cases.

---

[74]CalPERS has invested in Gatwick Airport, Indiana Tollroad, Port of Melbourne, and certain energy assets. CalSTRS has also made direct investments in infrastructure assets.

[75]Finite life funds are the typical structure for private equity strategies. Also referred to as closed-end funds, these have an "investment period" during which capital that has been committed to the fund by investors is drawn down and invested and then a "harvesting period" during which the value of investments is enhanced by the investment manager. All investments must be realized (sold) by the end of the fund's life although the investment manager may extend the fund life for a limited period, usually with consent of investors, in order to facilitate orderly realization of investments.

Table 3.3 shows the duration of funds to which the 25 largest public pension systems have made commitments, specifying the number of funds of each duration in which these pension systems have invested and the number of distinct commitments to funds of each duration.

Table 3.3: **Pension System Commitments to Infrastructure Funds by Duration (2007-2018)**

	Commitments	Distinct Funds
10-year	36	19
12-year	41	16
15-year	20	6
20-year	3	2
25-year	3	2
Other closed end (duration not disclosed)	103	59
Open-end	10	4
Listed	5	4

Source: Preqin. This table can be read as follows: In the case of funds with a 10-year duration, the 25 pension systems invested in 19 such funds through a total of 36 commitments.

Most of the funds to which the pension systems in our dataset have allocated are general infrastructure funds, although a substantial subset invests exclusively in energy infrastructure.[76]

Figure 3.1 shows the investment performance (net of fees) for funds of various duration, while Figure 3.2 presents investment performance of funds of various vintage years. It appears

---

[76]Of these funds, 123 are general infrastructure funds while 81 invest solely in energy infrastructure. The other funds invest in infrastructure debt or infrastructure secondaries or are funds-of-funds (i.e. they invest in fund interests as opposed to investing at the asset level). Many general infrastructure funds that invest in the U.S. have a bias towards power assets.

that longer-duration funds have performed better than shorter-duration funds.

Figure 3.1: **Pension System Commitments to Infrastructure Funds by Duration (2007-2018)**

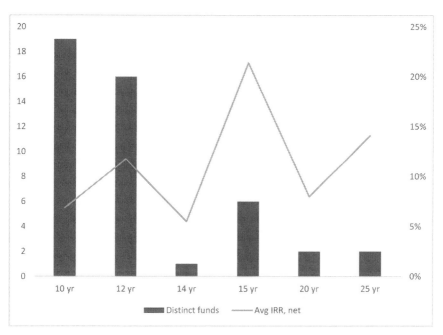

Source: Preqin.

Whereas the average fund earned a net IRR of 8.8% – above the average expected portfolio return of our sample of the 25 largest U.S. public pension systems – of the 37 infrastructure funds for which a target return range is reported, only nine exceeded the low end of that target. So, while finite-life funds have performed reasonably well, their performance has nevertheless fallen short of target.

Very little of the infrastructure investing by large pension systems has been through open-end funds.[77] Open-end funds generally hold assets for long periods, sometimes indefinitely, and generate most of their returns from current cash flows as opposed to capital appreciation. This kind of return stream is well matched to the needs of pension investors (Table 3.2). Among the infrastructure funds in which the top 25 public pension systems invested during the period covered by this study, there were only four open-end funds, three of which were sponsored by a single investment manager. All other exposures were through closed-end funds. These funds do not provide the cash-flow streams that pension investors indicate they are seeking as articulated in their investment policy statements (see Table 3.2).[78]

---

[77]Unlike finite-life funds, open-end funds are "evergreen" and have no set duration. Commitments by investors to these funds may be drawn down immediately, or may be "queued" and drawn down as soon as investment activity warrants capital infusions into the fund. Investments may be held for very long periods, or indefinitely. Investors seeking to redeem capital from the fund are generally placed into an exit queue and their redemption requests are satisfied once the investment manager obtains proceeds from realization of investments. In order to avoid realizations at inopportune points in market cycles, investment managers often have the option of "gating" or closing a fund to redemptions until such time as they deem it appropriate to sell investments. Investors then receive the proceeds for their redemption requests *pari passu* to others who have been placed into the exit queue.

[78]Andonov et al (2019) illustrate that finite-life infrastructure funds "deliver very similar payout profiles to traditional buyout private equity funds" and "do not provide more stable cash flows... than private equity funds".

Figure 3.2: **Pension System Commitments to Infrastructure Funds by Vintage Year (2007-2018)**

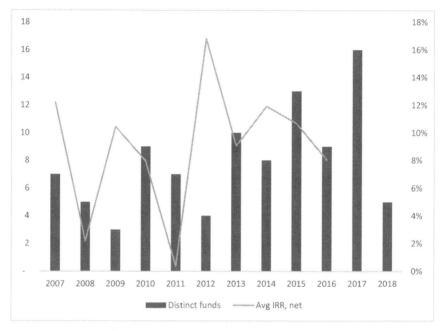

Source: Preqin.[79]

---

[79]The five funds with a 2008 vintage include one with a negative IRR, while the seven funds with a 2011 vintage include two with unreported IRRs and two with negative IRRs. Private equity style funds deliver negative returns in their early years when fund fees are levied based on committed capital. During that period, capital is not yet fully deployed into investments and investments have not yet had a chance to increase in value. This is known as the "J curve" and may partially explain the weaker performance of funds with 2015 and 2016 vintage.

4
Investment Performance of Infrastructure as an Asset Class

We next assess the performance of infrastructure investments on an absolute basis and relative to other asset classes. Our analysis pertains to performance of infrastructure as an asset class, not specifically in the portfolios of the top 25 public pension systems. The objective is to explore whether infrastructure tends to deliver the portfolio benefits that these institutional investors seek from their allocations to this asset class.

Private market equity infrastructure investing is a relatively new activity for large institutional asset managers like pension funds, particularly in the United States.[80] To evaluate the performance of private market infrastructure as an asset class, we use the MSCI Global Quarterly Infrastructure Index, which measures the performance of equity investments in infrastructure assets. The index was first issued in 2014 and comprises time series data beginning in March 2008. Our analysis is therefore based on 40 distinct quarterly observations.[81]

---

[80] With two exceptions, the top 25 U.S. public pension plans with active infrastructure programs established those programs between 2003 and 2009.

[81] Certain analyses in this section begin in 2009 to ensure complete data series.

The index is decomposed into various sub-indexes. For our purposes, we make limited reference to two of these – transport and power infrastructure investments. The index bifurcates the return on infrastructure investments into current income and capital return.[82] This index is the best available for our purposes,[83] but it has some drawbacks:

- **Fee drag**. As an asset-level index, it does not account for fees paid to investment managers. This affects its comparability with indexes for other asset classes that are reported on a fund-level, after-fee basis.[84] To reemphasize, fees are important because they embody a high level of certainty as against the return distribution on assets. However, correlations (a key part of our study) are not impacted directionally by fees.

- **Geographic bias**. The index is weighted to Australian and European infrastructure assets because of the portfolios held by reporting index contributors.[85] Many of the U.S. public pension systems invest in funds that exhibit a home-country bias.

- **Fund structure and investment strategy**. The funds that report to MSCI are open-end in structure, while al-

---

[82]It also reports separately returns for contracted and uncontracted assets.

[83]Another infrastructure index, measured at the fund level and published by an investment consulting firm is not released publicly and hence not used in our study.

[84]While MSCI publishes a fund-level after-fee index, that index is entirely comprised of Australia-domiciled funds and is heavily weighted (59%) to Australia-domiciled assets.

[85]As at December 2017, Australia-domiciled assets accounted for 45% of the index value, while European assets accounted for 42%. North America accounted for 10% of assets and New Zealand, 3%.

most all investing by U.S. public pension systems is in finite life funds, as noted earlier (Table 3.3).

- **Breadth.** The index comprised 113 assets from 11 data contributors at the end of the time series, which may not be adequately representative of the global infrastructure finance market.

Keeping in mind these caveats, we report how infrastructure has performed relative to the objectives articulated in pension plan investment policy statements (Table 3.2) – specifically inflation protection, portfolio diversification, stability of cash flows and risk-adjusted returns.

4.1 Inflation Protection

Figure 4.1 shows correlations between the total return of various asset classes and inflation, as reflected by the U.S. Consumer Price Index.[86] The MSCI index and the underlying component indexes for power and transport do not reveal inflation correlation.

---

[86]U.S. CPI is the most appropriate inflation measure since it is the benchmark for calculation of cost of living adjustments that apply to benefits provided by many public pension systems.

Figure 4.1: **Correlation of Asset Class Total Returns to U.S. CPI (2008-2017)**

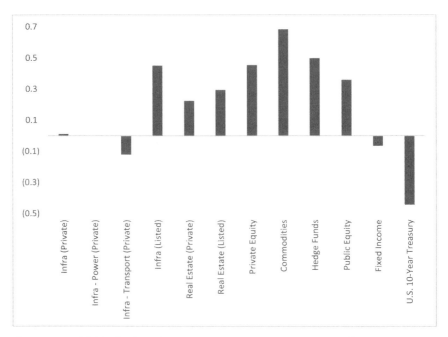

Sources: MSCI Global Quarterly Infrastructure Index (private infrastructure), DJ Brookfield Global Infrastructure Composite Index (listed infrastructure), MSCI Global Quarterly Property Fund Index, S&P U.S. REIT index (listed real estate), Cambridge Associates Buyout & Growth Equity Index (private equity), DJ Commodity Index (commodities), HFRX Aggregate Index (hedge funds), MSCI All Country World Index (public equity), Barclays Global Aggregate Bond Index (fixed income), U.S. 10-year U.S. Treasuries, Bureau of Labor Statistics (U.S. Consumer Price Index). Correlation based on quarterly data with no time lag. Private Infrastructure data is gross of fees.

Figure 4.2, which strips out capital returns – thereby isolating current income – indicates that the index and its constituents show negative inflation correlation. These results are both counterintuitive and contrary to the hypothesis contained in pension system investment policy statements.

What are we to make of this? We believe that four factors may be at play here. There has been limited inflation over the decade covered by our study. Additionally, the return stream on infrastructure has been very stable over the covered period, as shown in Figure 4.3, and this may have dominated any inflation correlation. Inflation resets, if any, may be different in geographies associated with funds included in the MSCI Index. Finally, there are probably delays between CPI observations and rate-resets that drive infrastructure cash flows.

Figure 4.2: **Correlation of Asset Class Income Returns to U.S. CPI (2008-2017)**

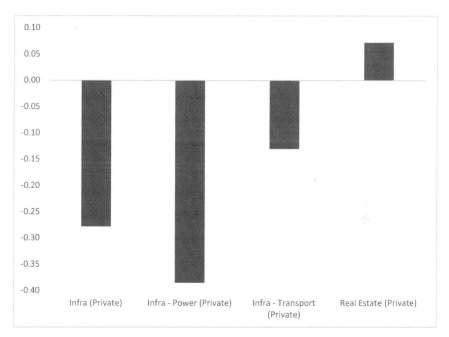

Sources: MSCI Global Quarterly Infrastructure Index (private infrastructure), MSCI Global Quarterly Property Index. Bureau of Labor Statistics (U.S. Consumer Price Index). Correlation based on quarterly data with no time lag. Private Infrastructure data is gross of fees.

In a more inflationary environment, one in which asset valuations are more volatile, the infrastructure return correlation could be quite different. So using this asset class as an inflation hedge over very long cycles may make sense.

4.2   Portfolio Diversification

The matrix in Table 4.1 compares infrastructure returns with those of other asset classes typically included in institutional investor portfolios. The data support the objective of portfolio diversification, with very low correlations between private market infrastructure and the other asset classes shown in the table. Private market infrastructure also has very low correlation with listed infrastructure, suggesting that listed infrastructure is not a good, liquid proxy for private market infrastructure. Instead, the correlation between listed infrastructure and public equity markets may dominate any correlation between listed and private market infrastructure.

Table 4.1: **Correlation Matrix of Asset Classes (Quarterly Total Return Data, 2009-2017)**

	Infrastructure (Private)	Infrastructure (Listed)	Real Estate (Private)	Real Estate (Listed)	Private Equity	Commodities	Hedge Funds	Public Equity	Fixed Income	U.S. 10-year Treasury	U.S. CPI
Infrastructure (Private)	1.00	~	~	~	~	~	~	~	~	~	~
Infrastructure (Listed)	0.00	1.00	~	~	~	~	~	~	~	~	~
Real Estate (Private)	0.42	0.20	1.00	~	~	~	~	~	~	~	~
Real Estate (Listed)	-0.04	0.73	0.30	1.00	~	~	~	~	~	~	~
Private Equity	0.19	0.80	0.50	0.66	1.00	~	~	~	~	~	~
Commodities	0.07	0.73	0.13	0.51	0.73	1.00	~	~	~	~	~
Hedge Funds	0.04	0.82	0.17	0.53	0.86	0.77	1.00	~	~	~	~
Public Equity	-0.06	0.87	0.19	0.74	0.87	0.71	0.90	1.00	~	~	~
Fixed Income	-0.24	0.42	-0.14	0.26	0.15	0.16	0.14	0.30	1.00	~	~
U.S. 10-year Treasury	-0.09	-0.36	-0.09	-0.29	-0.60	-0.59	-0.65	-0.59	0.45	1.00	~
U.S. CPI	0.01	0.45	0.22	0.29	0.45	0.68	0.50	0.36	-0.06	-0.44	1.00

Sources: MSCI Global Quarterly Infrastructure Index (private infrastructure), DJ Brookfield Global Infrastructure Composite Index (listed infrastructure), MSCI Global Quarterly Property Fund Index, S&P U.S. REIT index (listed real estate), Cambridge Associates Buyout & Growth Equity Index (private equity), DJ Commodity Index (commodities), HFRX Aggregate Index (hedge funds), MSCI All Country World Index (public equity), Barclays Global Aggregate Bond Index (fixed income), U.S. 10-year U.S. Treasuries, Bureau of Labor Statistics (U.S. Consumer Price Index). Correlation based on quarterly data with no time lag. Private Infrastructure data is gross of fees.

4.3 Stability of Cash Flows

Figure 4.3 shows the quarterly returns of private market infrastructure bifurcated between current income and capital return. The data strongly support the assertion that infrastructure assets generate stable cash flows. With yield (largely contracted) representing a significant portion of total returns, the asset class constitutes a defensive investment. Total returns were positive for all quarters during the period 2009-2017.

Figure 4.3: **Annual Return on Infrastructure by Quarterly Periods (2009- 2017)**

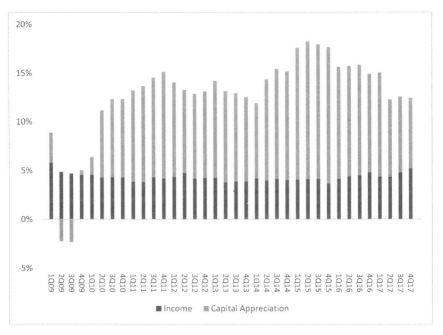

Source: MSCI Global Quarterly Infrastructure Index.

4.4 Risk-Adjusted Returns

Figure 4.4 shows the Sharpe Ratio of infrastructure investments and that of other asset classes, while Figure 4.5 maps the return and volatility of each of these asset classes. The observed Sharpe Ratio is unrealistically high for reasons we explain below. Nevertheless, for some investors, infrastructure has been a high-performing asset class even on an after-fee basis.[87]

---

[87]For example, CalPERS reported that infrastructure has been its best performing asset class over the year-ended June 30, 2018 (https://www.calpers.ca.gov/page/newsroom/calpers-news/2018/preliminary-fiscal-year-investment-returns) and over a five-year

Figure 4.4: **Risk-Adjusted Returns of Asset Classes (Sharpe Ratio)**

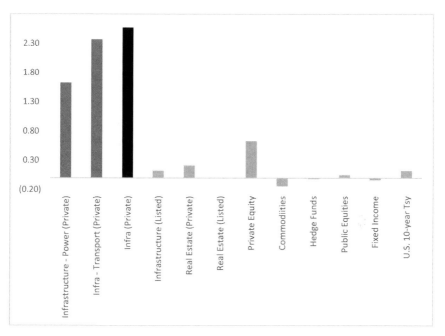

Sources: MSCI Global Quarterly Infrastructure Index (private infrastructure), DJ Brookfield Global Infrastructure Composite Index (listed infrastructure), MSCI Global Quarterly Property Fund Index, S&P U.S. REIT index (listed real estate), Cambridge Associates Buyout & Growth Equity Index (private equity), DJ Commodity Index (commodities), HFRX Aggregate Index (hedge funds), MSCI All Country World Index (public equity), Barclays Global Aggregate Bond Index (fixed income), U.S. 10-year U.S. Treasuries, Bureau of Labor Statistics (U.S. Consumer Price Index). Private Infrastructure data is gross of fees. Calculations based on quarterly observations over 10 years ending December 31, 2017.

Some of the Sharpe Ratio observations can be attributed to

---

period ending June 30, 2017 (https://www.calpers.ca.gov/docs/forms-publications/cio-performance-report-aug-2017.pdf).

an inconsistency in our analysis, since the available data measures infrastructure returns on a pre-fee basis whereas all of the other asset classes are evaluated on an after-fee basis.

The cumulative quarterly total return stream for infrastructure (Figure 4.6) depicts what appears to be unrealistically low volatility, which could explain the high observed Sharpe Ratio. We believe two factors may be at play here.

- **Supply of capital.** Over the 10-year period of analysis, infrastructure funds have seen substantial inflows that have exceeded growth in demand for private infrastructure capital. This has led to a growing mountain of "dry powder"[88] – dedicated investable funds committed and seeking to be deployed. One effect of this supply/demand imbalance has been that transactions have been executed at higher valuation levels.[89] It is particularly challenging to find reliable valuation metrics for private market infrastructure investments. A report issued by a manager of listed infrastructure funds suggests an average enterprise value-to-EBITDA multiple for a sample of ten large private infrastructure assets (airports, gas pipelines, and toll roads) of 19.4x as at September 30, 2017.[90] This is very high relative to private equity transactions, which were executed at an aver-

---

[88]Preqin estimated dry powder at $158 billion at December 31, 2017 and $179 billion at June 30, 2018, while the unrealized value of investments held by private infrastructure funds was $289 billion and $312 billion at those dates, respectively. These figures have doubled over a period of five years. They stood at $75 billion and $146 billion, respectively, at December 30, 2012.

[89]It has also resulted in an expansion in the definition of "infrastructure" as fund managers have sought out transactions in which to invest their fund commitments.

[90]Cohen & Steers, "The $150B Backlog Supporting Listed Infrastructure Valuations" (November 2017).

age EBITDA multiple of 11.3x at September 30, 2017.[91] *Ex post*, higher valuations increase the numerator in the Sharpe Ratio and may have caused some investors to be cautious about increasing allocations to the infrastructure asset class.[92]

- **Mark-to-market accounting.** Much of the value created by infrastructure funds is based on mark-to-market valuations as opposed to realization of investments.[93] During the holding period for these investments, quarterly valuations are based on appraisals, which are tied to valuations of precedent transactions. This is particularly true in the case of open-end funds as well as closed-end funds with vintage years of 2009 or later[94] and may plausibly explain lower levels of intra-year volatility in valuations, reducing the denominator in the Sharpe Ratio.

---

[91]Bain & Company, Global Private Equity Report 2018, p. 5.

[92]An investment officer for the Florida Retirement System reported to its investment council, "We think that there is an imbalance of demand over supply for attractive risk-adjusted returns. So we really haven't been doing a whole lot in infrastructure over the last few years." (State Board of Administration of Florida, Investment Advisory Council Meeting, December 4, 2017: https://www.sbafla.com/fsb/Portals/FSB/Content/IAC/2018/20180319_IAC_Agenda_And_Meeting_Materials.pdf)

[93]Infrastructure assets are held for reasonably long periods of time, which is true for closed-end funds and is even more true for open-end funds of the type that are included in the index.

[94]These funds typically have substantial value in unrealized investments.

Figure 4.5: **Risk and Return of Asset Classes (2008-2017)**

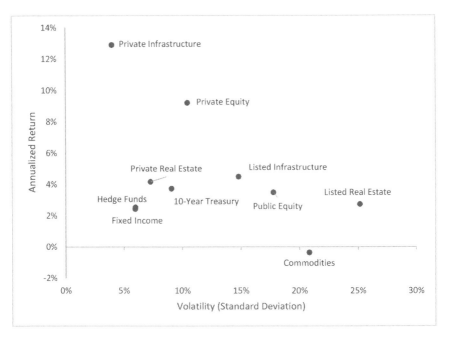

Sources: MSCI Global Quarterly Infrastructure Index (private infras-tructure), DJ Brookfield Global Infrastructure Composite Index (listed infrastructure), MSCI Global Quarterly Property Fund Index, S&P U.S. REIT index (listed real estate), Cambridge Associates Buyout & Growth Equity Index (private equity), DJ Commodity Index (com-modities), HFRX Aggregate Index (hedge funds), MSCI All Country World Index (public equity), Barclays Global Aggregate Bond Index (fixed income), U.S. 10-year U.S. Treasuries, Bureau of Labor Statis-tics (U.S. Consumer Price Index). Private Infrastructure data is gross of fees.

Figure 4.6 shows the cumulative quarterly total returns of each asset class. As we have noted, the observation for the MSCI index is not comparable with that of other asset classes as it is reported on an asset-level basis (not on a net-of-expenses fund-level basis).

Figure 4.6: **Cumulative Quarterly Total Returns of Asset Classes (2008- 2017)**

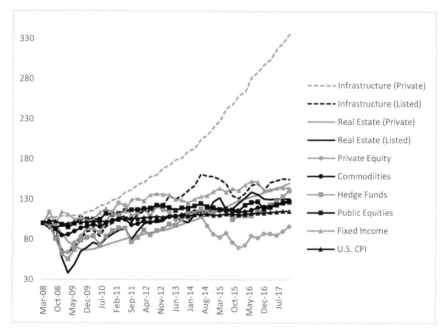

Sources: see Figure 4.5. The data behind this chart suffers from an inherent distortion in that the MSCI index, which is used to represent private infrastructure, reports investment returns on an asset level basis such that investment expenses are not deducted from investment returns. The other investable asset classes (listed infrastructure, private and listed real estate, private equity, and hedge funds) are reported on a fund level and hence on an after-fee basis.

5
The Road Ahead

What are the implications of our study for public pension systems and the investment managers who market their intermediation services to these pension systems?

5.1 Enhanced Governance of Public Pension Systems

We have observed a number of areas in which the governance of public pensions could be enhanced, among these are the following:

- **Composition of boards of trustees**. Pension boards are generally comprised of representatives of pension beneficiaries, the general public, and sponsoring public entities. One of the most important duties of the board of a public pension system is oversight of the investing program. While relevant professional experience is seldom a prerequisite to board participation, efforts should be made to ensure that boards include sufficient representation of trustees with investing, finance, and actuarial experience. All trustees should receive appropriate and ongoing training.

- **ADEC funding discipline**. There is a positive relationship between the degree to which public sector employers fund contributions and the funded status of public pension plans. Discretion over ADEC funding is a weakness of plan governance. Rules (even legislation) requiring pension funding – at least over a rolling period of several years – should be put in place and enforced to preempt intergenerational inequity.

- **Benefit transparency**. Our study has not entered into the debate about pension benefit levels or the way in which benefits are determined. There are inherent conflicts in this process because benefit levels are the result of negotiations between labor (beneficiaries) and employers (public sector officials). One group is highly organized, the other transient. One is focused on long-term benefits, the other reluctant to take a very long-term perspective. And of course, only one group has voting power. Ultimately, there should be greater transparency – and accountability – as to pension benefit policy and the process by benefits are determined.

- **Voice of the taxpayer**. Pension obligations are well protected in law such that the ultimate "at risk" stakeholder for public pensions is the taxpayer, not the plan beneficiary. And yet the taxpayer has no direct voice in pension governance. Pension solvency is a function of numerous factors, including the level of benefits and employee contributions, tax policy, funding discipline, sophistication of the investment program, active expense management, and transparency in pension accounting. Consequently, it is the responsibility of the public to be better informed about the factors that impact pension funding and demand of its elected officials – and their representatives on pension boards – greater transparency and enhanced governance in all aspects of operating public pension systems.

- **Uniformity in determining expected investment re-**

turns. The discount rate is the single most important variable in determining pension funded status. It is based on the expected return of the investment portfolio which itself is based on the asset allocation and long-term expected returns by asset class. While portfolios are constructed in bespoke ways and different projections are to be expected, we have illustrated that there is little uniformity in expected returns by asset class. It would be beneficial to pension governance for there to be clear guidance and greater uniformity as to the time horizon, asset class definition[95] and benchmark selection for various asset classes. This point applies equally to inflation projections that form part of the discount rate calculus.

- **Liability and cash flow-sensitive investment management**. Investment gains and income provide approximately two-thirds of the cash-flows that fund pension obligations, yet these are by far the most volatile of the sources of pension cash flows. Reducing this volatility is important, as is investing with a liability-aware approach. We have illustrated that funded status impacts asset allocation, but that asset allocation does not clearly correlate to net investment returns. This suggests that pension systems with greater allocation to riskier assets may not be rewarded for these allocations. This argues for modes of investing that more directly address balance sheet and cash flow needs of pension plans.

- **Enhanced expense reporting**. Pension fund accounting should require more comprehensive reporting of all external

---

[95] Overly rigid asset class definitions are, however, equally problematic as they may result in institutional investors passing on what might otherwise be good investment opportunities because they do not fit within tightly-defined asset class boundaries. A more sophisticated approach would be to measure every asset on a risk-parity – or similar – basis without any asset class limitations.

investment expenses along with clear guidelines as to how
these expenses should be reported. Internal investment-
related expenses should also be disclosed. Ultimately, this
will lead to greater transparency as to the expense ratio of
pension systems and allow pension administrators to balance the overall mix of investing activity between internal
and external sources.

- **Active expense management**. A critical factor for public pension systems is to reduce investment management
  expenses. Compounded high expenses will – if unaddressed
  – turn out to be a significant burden on future taxpayers.
  This issue has received increasing scrutiny among institutional investors and the public sector officials who oversee
  pension systems. Notable is the case of Pennsylvania where
  the State Treasurer established a commission to review the
  management of the state's public pension systems. The
  commission issued a report[96] in December 2018 that included several recommendations directly pertaining to investment expenses, including fully indexing public market
  investments, combining the investment offices of the state's
  two large public pension systems, and greater transparency
  on investment expenses.[97] These recommendations may
  not be the right ones for every pension system – or even
  for those in Pennsylvania – but increased attention on this
  topic is likely to continue.

---

[96]https://www.patreasury.gov/pdf/2018-PPMAIRC-FINAL.pdf. The
expected response by the administrators of the Pennsylvania pension systems to the state commission's report had not been released at the time of
writing.

[97]Treasurers of several other states, including North Carolina and Rhode
Island have also made pension system investment expenses a policy priority.

5.2 The Continuum of Greater Control by Public Pension Systems

We noted at the beginning of this study that very few of the factors impacting public pension funding are subject to control by those who administer the systems. The levers that can be controlled by investment staff – asset allocation, security selection, and investment expenses – are limited.

As long-duration investors with limited need for liquidity beyond funding negative cash flows (excess of benefit payments over contributions), most pension systems have increasingly taken advantage of the illiquidity premia inherent in private assets.[98]

The substantial allocation of pension capital to private investment funds is subject to agency problems. The interests of investment managers who oversee these funds are not necessarily aligned with those of the client pension systems and their beneficiaries. Investment managers are incentivized to exit asset positions once value creation has been achieved, while pension investors may prefer to continue to hold assets for longer periods – perhaps indefinitely. And investment fund fees tend to be very high – arguably commensurate with the degree of skill involved and the competitive structure of the industry. Thus, investment expenses are a topic of increasing focus, particularly in the case of very large investment funds, as we have noted.

Some institutional investors have adopted, or are exploring, models in which they have greater control over their investment programs. These models involve a trade-off between greater con-

---

[98]While there are arguments that illiquidity premia decay over time and that premia may be due to the perceived benefits of smoothing, what is important here is that pension systems invest in illiquid assets believing that they will obtain a premium on such investments.

trol and customization with lower third-party expenses, on the one hand, and potentially lower expenses, but significant organizational disruption and reconfiguration on the other.

Clark et al (2011) detail necessary evolutional requirements for such internalization of investing, which include (i) clear expectations for the investment program in terms of risk and return, (ii) clarity in scope of the investment strategy, (iii) sufficiency of capital allocation in order to achieve the investment objectives, (iv) staffing across all functional areas of the investment, asset management, and support processes, including appropriate remuneration practices, (v) appropriate governance processes, and (iv) protocols that immunize decision-making from external influence.

The evolution from a traditional model of fund commitments to more direct models of investing can best be understood as a continuum:

- **Co-investing**. The investor secures rights to co-investments alongside a fund commitment. This facilitates some degree of customization over desired investment exposures along with more rapid deployment of capital and reduced total expenses. Co-investments are often offered at reduced fees or on a zero-fee basis. Co-investment rights are generally available only to large investors that make substantial fund commitments, and they are only applicable to sophisticated investors who can respond flexibly to new investment opportunities.

- **Customized investing**. A number of pension systems have established separately managed accounts with investment managers able to offer a diverse stream of investment exposures. These programs are usually undertaken for very large asset management commitments, and generally provide full discretion to the investment manager.[99] The advantage of these programs is that they establish a close relationship with a selected investment manager, facilitate priority access to investment opportunities, and benefit from reduced investment expenses.

- **Collaborative investing**. Monk et al (2015) discuss ways in which institutional investors collaborate to their collective benefit – through research clubs, roundtables,[100] and co-investment structures. This approach is particularly common among large single- and multi-family office investors. Among U.S. public pension systems, CalSTRS held a series of hearings in 2018 to explore the benefits of this model[101] and concluded that it could result in "increasing control and transparency, and... significant overall cost savings".[102] Likewise, CalPERS' investment consultant recommended that the pension system "explore club and consortia vehicles, such as joint ventures and other structures, with like-minded institutional investors".[103]

- **Consortium Investing**. There are some examples of groups of institutional investors establishing jointly-owned

---

[99]Among U.S. public pension systems, Texas Teachers is particularly notable in having established sizeable separately managed accounts.

[100]The authors cite examples of the Institutional Investors Roundtable, the Long-Term Investors Club, the Pacific Pension Institute, and the World Economic Forum's Long-Term Investment Council. They propose a position of Chief Networking Officer to help facilitate the full benefits of collaboration.

[101]See especially the February, September, and November sessions: https://www.calstrs.com/post/2018-board-meetings

[102]https://www.calstrs.com/sites/main/files/file-attachments/annualbudget_2018-19.pdf

[103]https://www.calpers.ca.gov/docs/board-agendas/201809/invest/item07d-02_a.pdf

investment managers to deploy capital on their behalf. For example – CalSTRS and Dutch pension fund APG established the Infrastructure Alliance Partnership, managed by Argo Infrastructure Partners.[104] While the particulars of these consortia may differ;[105] the objective is generally the same – to facilitate a greater degree of customization than is possible through conventional fund commitments, along with much lower investment expenses. Savings are shared by members of the investing consortium. An advantage of these consortia is that they operate at arms-length from, and are governed independently of, each of the owners. One benefit of that is the ability to compensate investment staff at levels above those that are typical for public sector staff of U.S. pension systems. This approach is appropriate for large, mid-size, and even small institutional investors. One concern is that it can be expected to run into complications in ensuring ongoing commonality of interest among participating investors.

- **Captive Investment Affiliates**. A small number of institutional investors have adopted a model of wholly-owned but independent investment affiliates. For example – in May 2018 CalPERS announced the establishment of

---

[104]CalSTRS and APG each committed $250 million to Argo's program, and announced in September 2018 that they would each commit an additional $300 million to this program.

[105]Other examples of consortia include (i) Industry Funds Management (IFM), a multi-asset class investment manager owned by a group of Australian superannuation funds, (ii) Local Pensions Partnership, which invests on behalf of the Lancashire County Council and the London Pensions Fund Authority, (iii) The Pension Infrastructure Platform, established by The Pension Protection Fund, The National Association of Pension Funds, and the UK Treasury, and (iv) Capital Constellation, established by the Alaska Permanent Fund, the Public Institution for Social Security of Kuwait and UK pension plan, RMPI RailPen.

CalPERS Direct,[106] to facilitate direct investing in two strategies – (i) late-stage investments in technology, life sciences, and healthcare, and (ii) long-term investments in established companies. This model allows the sponsoring institution to establish clear investment guidelines, remove key agency conflicts, and reduce investment expenses. Captive affiliates may be established *de novo* or they may be investment firms acquired by the institutional investor.[107]

- **Direct Investing**. The most sophisticated institutional investors have internalized all or substantial portions of their investment programs. While this allows for complete control over investment exposures, it places a substantial burden on the investor. It is appropriate only for the largest investors able to support the necessary fixed expense of establishing internal investment teams, and for the most sophisticated investors who can ensure the rigorous governance structures demanded by this approach. The Canada Pension Plan Investment Board (CPP IB) and many other Canadian public pension plans operate in this manner. While the cost of internal investing teams is substantial, so are the savings relative to continued allocation to third-party funds.[108] Direct investing also allows for

---

[106]CalPERS Direct will be governed independently of CalPERS. See: https://www.calpers.ca.gov/page/newsroom/calpers-news/2018/direct-investment-model-private-equity.

[107]A pioneer in use of the captive affiliate model is the Ontario Municipal Employees' Retirement System (OMERS), which has acquired two formerly independent investment managers to allocate capital exclusively on its behalf. Oxford Properties invests for OMERS in real estate, while OMERS Infrastructure (formerly – Borealis Infrastructure) invests in infrastructure. Among U.S. pension systems, Arizona Retirement System acquired a 50%-interest in Mill Creek Residential Trust in April 2018.

[108]CPP IB included the following observation pertaining to its infrastructure allocation in its 2016 annual report, "We estimate that the total

maximum customization of investment exposures so that each investment can be judged on its own merits – and on the benefit it will provide to the rest of the portfolio.[109] Very few among U.S. pension systems can wholly adopt in-house investing structures, although some are increasingly doing so with individual asset classes, such as public equities and fixed income.[110] We expect that this approach will be adopted over time for lower risk private capital strategies, at least in the case of the largest pension systems. This would be most applicable to strategies such as core real estate and core infrastructure which are characterized by the type of long-term perspective typical of a long duration investor. Certain strategies, such as corporate credit and private equity investing would be much less appropriate for pension systems in light of the type of value-creation

---

costs for an externally managed $15 billion of committed capital on average would range from $600 million to $700 million per year. By contrast, our fully costed internal management of our $21 billion infrastructure portfolio amounted to approximately $65 million." Likewise, Ashby Monk of Stanford University's Global Projects Center is quoted as saying about CalPERS' $689 million in private equity fees, "If you take 10% of that ($700 million) to fund a new team in an arm's length entity, it could do wonders... That's $70 million per year in compensation! You could build an incredible team with that. Now, take the remaining $630 million in savings and, every year, compound that savings at 7% (CalPERS' expected return). In 30 years, the value of the savings alone will be over $700 billion." (https://www.pionline.com/article/20180528/PRINT/180529850/california-pension-funds-on-separate-paths-to-direct-investment). Texas TRS is seeking to increase its investing team from 150 to 270 and grow internal management of its private capital portfolio from 20% to 30% in order to undertake more direct investing which would, according to its CIO, "cut external fund managers and slice fees by at least $600 million" (https://www.bloomberg.com/news/articles/2018-03-23/texas-teachers-pension-eyes-hiring-spree-for-investment-group).

[109]CPP IB refers to this approach as Total Portfolio Management.

[110]Pennsylvania PSERS, NCRS, and Texas TRS have all announced their intention to move more of their investing in-house.

strategies typical of investors in those areas, which would not be appropriate for a public fund investment office.

The argument here is not for disintermediation of investment managers, but rather that those pension systems for which it is appropriate, consider taking greater control over investing in order to obtain more customized exposures and reduce investment expenses. These are "make or buy" decisions and give rise to an array of advantages and disadvantages for pension systems and their beneficiaries. Moving along the Continuum of Greater Control can only be accomplished with substantial investment in governance, processes, and staffing. Staffing models for greater internal investment capabilities require larger teams with more investment experience. These changes are very disruptive and require compensation models that are not feasible for most public pension systems, which is why they can be expected to happen very slowly, if at all.

5.3 A Long-Duration Model for Investing in Infrastructure

We turn now to ways of matching pension capital with infrastructure financing needs. As we will illustrate, these two public finance disciplines are tightly connected. Pension funds seek long-duration investments, of which infrastructure is a prime example. Well-functioning infrastructure is essential to economic viability of the local, regional and national economy and hence to tax revenues. Tax revenues of course are an important factor in funding employer contributions. Likewise, pension capital is both substantial in size and patient in duration, each of which is important to infrastructure finance. The reverse relationship is likewise compelling – there have been examples of financing of pension funding deficits crowding out other public finance needs, including infrastructure development and maintenance.

Infrastructure evidences most – although not all – of the objectives articulated in the investment policy statements of U.S. public pension systems that allocate portfolio shares to the asset class. Structured through open-end funds, it has delivered diversification and predictable cash flows. While it has generated strong capital appreciation, levels of recent years may not be sustainable. However, very few U.S. public pension plans access infrastructure through open-end funds. Finite life funds are the norm. To reemphasize, this raises fundamental questions because the cash flows from finite life infrastructure funds are essentially driven by private-equity strategies that are not focused on long-duration predictable cash flows.

In respect of longer duration assets, this suggests that pension investors should press for – and investment managers should provide – access vehicles that facilitate longer-duration exposure to infrastructure. Open-end fund structures are common in real estate investment management where the underlying assets are long-duration holdings whose investment returns are primarily based on cash flows funded by lease payments. Similar cash flows apply in the case of certain infrastructure assets (especially those with long-term contracted revenue streams). At present, very few open-end infrastructure funds operate in the U.S. even though this is the structure most appropriate to the articulated needs of public pension systems. This is slowly changing. Pension funds should also seek this exposure in a more direct manner along the continuum just described. This type of longer-duration capital may also make it more likely for public sector procurement agencies to consider pension systems as financing partners in development and ownership of public infrastructure assets. We return to this topic below.

The key argument of fiduciary standards is that investments

of pension capital must be taken solely in the interests of plan beneficiaries. Directing pension capital to infrastructure development introduces political risk and potentially blurs the lines of fiduciary standards.[111]

However, there are externalities to consider in pension-financed infrastructure investments. It is fair to infer a positive correlation between the state of a region's infrastructure and the vitality of its economy. NYCERS, for example, has been encouraged to invest in sustainable infrastructure[112] and has a 2% allocation to "economically targeted investments" that are intended to promote economic development in New York City.[113] If infrastructure leads to job growth and a stronger tax base, that is ultimately good for pension systems. And as we have emphasized, the ultimate guarantor of pension solvency is the taxpayer. Infrastructure investments generate large external benefits that boost incomes and accelerate growth, which in turn reinforces the funding of public employee pensions and enhances the ability of pension systems to meet obligations as well as bolstering taxpayers' ability to backstop any shortfalls. Done right, this encourages a virtuous circle.

---

[111]Mitchell & Yang (2005) reference an earlier study which found that "economically targeted investments... were associated with lower investment returns." Though not a greenfield project, the 2011 transfer of the Queensland Motorway from the State of Queensland to QIC, an Australian superannuation fund manager owned by the Queensland government, by way of a 40-year concession, is illustrative of this tension. Bennon et al (2017) describe this in-kind contribution from a state to a pension system and highlight the necessity of the buyer being highly sophisticated and the transaction being done at "arm's length, without political influence."

[112]https://comptroller.nyc.gov/wp-content/uploads/documents/1-25-2018-Common-Investment-Meeting-NYCERS-Public.pdf.

[113]https://comptroller.nyc.gov/services/financial-matters/pension/initiatives/economically-targeted-investments/.

5.4 Increasing the Size of Infrastructure Allocations

The average infrastructure allocation among the 25 largest public pension systems in the U.S. is less than 1% (Table 3.1). Real assets as a whole account for a growing portion of public pension plan portfolios (Figure 2.17) and infrastructure is an important – though small – component of this category. Yet it provides distinct benefits for pension portfolios, and can be expected to become a more prominent investment component.

It is instructive to compare U.S. pension infrastructure allocations with those of the large Canadian public pension plans (Table 5.1). Canadian plans define infrastructure as a dedicated asset class and have been allocating meaningfully to infrastructure for many years. They do most of their investing on a direct basis. It is worth noting that Australian superannuation funds have also developed substantial infrastructure investment portfolios. If infrastructure continues to deliver the cash flows that we have illustrated in Figure 4.3, it is reasonable to argue that allocations to the asset class should be materially increased among major pension funds in the United States, subject to supply/demand considerations noted below.[114]

---

[114]CalSTRS was reported in September 2018 to be considering doubling its target allocation for infrastructure from 2% to 4% (https://www.ft.com/content/d3248e44-bc6b-32b1-b93c-bc455f42a1cf).

Table 5.1: Canadian Public Pension Plan Infrastructure Investments

	Net Assets (C$ Million)	Infrastructure Investments (C$ Million)	Percentage Allocation
Canada Pension Plan	356,134	30,399	7.1%
Ontario Teachers' Pension Plan	189,480	18,740	10.1%
Public Service Pension Plan	112,276	12,949	10.2%
Ontario Municipal Employees Retirement System	95,198	15,679	16.3%
Healthcare of Ontario Pension Plan	77,755	-	0.0%
Municipal Pension Plan of British Columbia	43,145	4,533	10.4%
Local Authorities Pension Plan of Alberta	42,729	3,069	7.2%
Ontario Pension Board	26,482	1,435	5.4%
British Columbia Public Service Pension Plan	23,818	2,436	10.3%
British Columbia Teachers' Pension Plan	22,919	2,343	10.2%

Source: Annual Reports. Excludes Quebec pension plans. All data as of December 31, 2017 except for Canada Pension Plan, Public Service Pension Plan, and British Columbia Public Service Pension Plan, for which data is as of March 31, 2018. Data for British Columbia pension plans is in respect of Basic Account only (excludes Inflation Index Account) and Infrastructure investments for these portfolios includes Renewables investments. Percentage allocation is calculated relative to total portfolio assets (including leverage), not relative to net assets.

Figure 5.1 compares the 25 largest U.S. public pension systems with their 10 largest Canadian peers from the perspective of assets under management and infrastructure allocations. With one exception, the Canadian plans all have substantially larger portions of their portfolios allocated to infrastructure investments. This is particularly noteworthy in the case of the five largest Canadian pension plans, which are of a similar size to the U.S. peer group. This may be explained by a number of factors, including an earlier start to investing in infrastructure and the ability to invest directly into infrastructure assets on a global basis using in-house teams of captive investment affiliates.

Figure 5.1: **Infrastructure in U.S. and Canadian Public Pension Plan Portfolios**

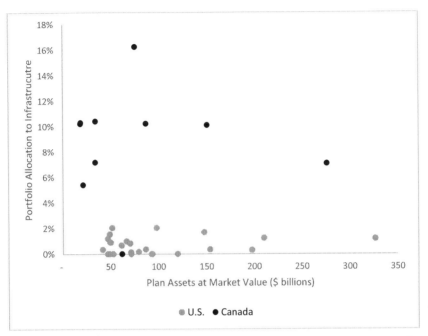

Source: Annual Reports. Canadian pension plan assets converted to U.S. dollars at exchange rate in effect at fiscal year-end of each plan. Plan assets reported net of portfolio leverage.

5.5 Pension Capital and Infrastructure Development

Increased allocations to infrastructure should be considered from the perspective of both supply of and demand for capital. This leads to the question of whether pension capital can or should be used to stimulate infrastructure development. Common sense suggests that large, capital-intensive, long-duration assets that generate major positive economic and social externalities should be financed from pools of investable capital requiring long-duration, high credit quality and significant cash-flows. Creation of an efficient pipeline between pension assets and infrastructure capital needs is compelling and has long been applied in a number of countries.

But in the United States, most publicly-operated infrastructure has been financed using state and local municipal or "muni" debt. The tax-exempt features of this debt make it unattractive for pension funds, with the result that the largest single pool of investable capital in the country does not find its way to significant financing of critical U.S. infrastructure. Moreover, the cost of pension capital (i.e. the investment returns expected by pension investors) exceeds the cost of muni debt, so public sector procurement agencies will prefer the cheaper debt to more expensive private capital, including that of pension investors, absent structural incentives.

On the positive side, growth in capital needs for infrastructure and pressures on public sector finances have led to increased focus on the role that pension capital might play in financing infrastructure development. In 2011, CalPERS held a series of roundtables to explore the "role CalPERS and other pension systems can play in facilitating infrastructure investment in California".[115] Certainly, political influence on investment management is a concern for plan fiduciaries. But this does raise the question of whether pension systems should include societal[116] and economic benefits in the calculus of evaluating investments

---

[115]https://www.calpers.ca.gov/docs/forms-publications/infrastructure-investment-outreach.pdf.

[116]Our discussion here does not refer to the growing trend towards environmental- social-governance (ESG) sensitivity in infrastructure investing, although that is a topic that has begun impacting the way that pension systems think about infrastructure. For example, CalPERS is a founding member of GRESB Infrastructure (https://gresb.com/gresb-infrastructure/), which focuses on this very point.

in infrastructure, particularly repurposing brownfield infrastructure and developing greenfield infrastructure.

Dachis (2017) and Cooper and Craig (2013) explore this topic, in the context of public-private partnerships, federally-subsidized taxable bonds, federal loan guarantees, and credit enhancements that might make infrastructure bonds appropriate for tax exempt investors.[117]

5.6 Greenfield Development

What about financing of new infrastructure development?

There are scattered examples in the United States of pension systems having invested directly in infrastructure development projects. In 2009, the Dallas Police & Fire Pension System invested in development of a Texas expressway[118] and in 2012, Cal-

---

[117]Existing programs include the Transportation Infrastructure Finance and Innovation Act (TIFIA), the Water Infrastructure Finance and Innovation Act (WIFIA) and the Railroad Rehabilitation and Financing program (RRIF), all of which provide some form of loan guarantee or credit subsidy.

[118]The press release announcing this investment included the following quotation from the pension plan's administrator, "We believe that the DPFPS is the first U.S. pension fund in the country to invest in the building and maintenance of a major toll road infrastructure project like the North Tarrant Express... It's an excellent investment for our 8,500 members and their families and a vital investment in our community. As available public resources for highway projects have dwindled, it's private investment by our own citizens like the DPFPS that will build the roads and highways in our communities. We believe that private investment is the future model for infrastructure construction in this country. It's a visionary move by our leadership to be the first pension fund to participate, and a win-win-win for the citizens of the Dallas-Fort Worth Metroplex." More recently, this pension system has experienced serious cash flow challenges. In May 2017, it was reported to be exiting this investment to use the proceeds to alleviate these problems. In October 2018, it announced that it would completely exit the

STRS committed \$42.8 million to four California infrastructure projects.[119] These involve pension-system financing of greenfield infrastructure development with the objective of ultimately owning and operating the asset.

The risks (and cash flows) associated with greenfield development[120] are substantially different from those associated with owning an operating asset, and investors bifurcate their exposure to such transactions between higher-risk development exposure and lower-risk operating exposure.

Can institutional investors reduce the risk associated with greenfield development? Two factors can be considered.

- **Superior insight**. For sophisticated investors, in the case of geographies or assets that are particularly well-known to them, the associated risk reduction may be compelling. It may explain the role of Quebec pension plan, CDPQ, in the financing and operation of Montreal's light rail system.

- **Partnership with EPC firms**. Pension systems investing directly in greenfield projects could do so along with engineering-procurement-construction (EPC) firms. These

---

infrastructure asset class, based on guidance of its investment consultant.

[119]In CalSTRS' press release announcing these transactions, the chairman of its investment committee noted, "These investments reflect CalSTRS' commitment to the California economy and our willingness to contribute to it in a way that helps our state and offers the fund long-term, steady cash flows. The construction projects, in particular, will put more than 600 Californians to work... We will continue to actively seek out greater investment opportunities in California infrastructure that meet our program objectives," https://www.calstrs.com/news-release/calstrs-announces-california-infrastructure-investments

[120]Greenfield investing is conceptually riskier than buying existing assets because of uncertainties related to future revenues as well as the potential for budget overruns related to both cost and time of project development.

firms bring extensive experience in the design and construction of prior projects. Bennon et al (2015) illustrate the investment by Dutch pension funds PGGM and APG alongside EPC operator BAM in the development of the N33 road-widening project in the Netherlands.

5.7 Asset Recycling

An innovative way pension capital can be used to help with the financing of infrastructure development is through the asset recycling model common in Australia. Under this approach, long-term concessions on infrastructure assets are sold to investors, including pension funds, while the proceeds are used by the public sector to invest in new development. The public sector retains ownership over legacy assets, the pension investor obtains access to proven long-duration cash flows, and the development and operating risk on new infrastructure is retained by the public sector procurement agency.

5.8   Public-Private Partnerships

Public-private partnerships ("P3s")[121] are the subject of growing attention as a model for the financing of public infrastructure. While quite common in other countries, P3s are still at a nascent stage in the U.S. This is partly due to the well-functioning municipal bond market, as previously discussed. However, the P3 industry has actively promoted ancillary benefits. These include the transfer of risk away from public agencies and the need to consider full life-cycle costs of operating infrastructure facilities, not just the upfront capital expenditures to develop these projects. Interest in P3s as a source of financing is also driven by fiscal constraints facing many states, municipalities, and public agencies that are unable to tap bond markets as readily as they had in the past.

The absence of uniformity in P3 legislation across the country (enabling legislation to support P3s does not exist in many states), the highly customized nature of concession agreements, and oversight responsibilities to monitor the operation of P3 relationships, act as additional inhibitors in the adoption of P3s.

---

[121]Public-private partnerships are contractual agreements between public and private sector entities pursuant to which the private sector plays a role in the delivery of public services. In the infrastructure context, this can take the form of private sector involvement in the design, build, financing, operation, or maintenance of infrastructure assets. This is commonly referenced by the acronym DBFOM or some form thereof for models that do not entail all five components. For purposes of our discussion, we are particularly interested in the private financing of public infrastructure through generally long-term concession agreements under which private investors acquire the rights to future cash flows from an infrastructure asset. These cash-flows can be (i) volume based and paid by users (for example – tolls), (ii) volume based and paid by a public agency (shadow tolls), or (iii) transfers not dependent on volume but on satisfactory service levels (availability payments). Direct tolling is less common in the U.S. than it is in many other countries, an impediment to the adoption of P3s.

With governmental entities as counterparties, investors in P3s are exposed to political risk that ranges from failure to approve concession agreements to early termination.

Another obstacle to the broader use of P3s is the experience with cost overruns on large scale projects. This has led several highly capable EPC companies – to whom excess risk has been assigned on such procurements – to exit this market.[122]

Nevertheless, in a well-functioning P3 environment, public pension plans should be viewed as a potentially robust source of infrastructure capital. Beyond the scale and patient nature of pension fund balance sheets are two other factors.

First, where opposition to P3s emanates from concerns about transferring public assets to private investors (particularly from labor unions), this issue is mitigated when the source of capital is the pension assets of public sector workers.

Second, recent enhancements to the oversight role of the Committee on Foreign Investment in the United States (CFIUS)[123] with respect to foreign investment in American infrastructure

---

[122]For a recent example, see: Campo-Flores, A and Overberg, P (2019, May 29). The Interstate is Crumbling. Try Fixing the Section Used by 200,000 Vehicles a Day. *Wall Street Journal.*

[123]CFIUS is an interagency committee of Congress that reviews national security considerations pertaining to foreign investments in the U.S. See here for more detail: https://home.treasury.gov/policy-issues/international/the-committee-on-foreign-investment-in-the-united-states-cfius. The Foreign Investment Risk Review Modernization Act of 2018 (FIRRMA) expanded the jurisdiction of CFIUS to address "the potential national security-related effects of the cumulative control of... any one type of critical infrastructure, energy asset, critical material, or critical technology by a foreign government or foreign person".

also favor public pension plans relative to other large pools of patient capital such as sovereign wealth funds and non-U.S. pension funds.

Certainly, very few – if any – U.S. public pension investment offices are capable of deploying capital directly into P3s without the involvement of a specialist investment firm as an intermediary. For this reason, pension capital for infrastructure depends on wider adoption of the P3 model by the investment management industry.

Many sponsors of infrastructure investment funds have been circumspect about entering the P3 market because of the complexities associated with these transactions and because of the relatively small equity component in the capital structure of P3 financings. That said, each new and successful P3 transaction adds to the body of evidence favoring this form of financing and a critical mass of successful transactions could introduce a tipping point beyond which P3s become a more common form of infrastructure finance.

5.9 Innovations in Infrastructure Finance

In addition to P3s, there are other creative financing models to match pension capital with infrastructure financing needs.

One of these is the concept of "value capture." Land appreciates significantly in value once it is serviced by infrastructure and accessible for commercial development. This is particularly true with respect to transportation infrastructure, but applies to other types of infrastructure – public and social – as well. Value capture directly and indirectly ties the increase in land values to the infrastructure that makes land more valuable. Future tax revenues from properties on land serviced by new infrastructure can be securitized, and the bond proceeds can be used to pay for the infrastructure.[124] Value capture can also be structured to use the proceeds from the sale of development rights on land serviced by new infrastructure to finance the infrastructure itself.[125] One way in which public pension capital can leverage value capture techniques is through the establishment of investment structures that essentially "staple" infrastructure and property developments. These are both long-duration investment strategies, and each benefits the other. As noted earlier, pension investment offices would generally be unable to structure this type of financing directly. Rather, it would be necessary to introduce a financial intermediary to operate such structure on behalf one or more pension systems.

Availability payment structures and creative use of value capture are options for the use of private capital or public pension capital for the financing of infrastructure where there is no obvious revenue stream.

---

[124]This model is essentially what was used to finance the extension of New York City's subway system to the Hudson Yards district.

[125]This model has been widely used to finance expansion of Hong Kong's MTR transit system, where it is referred to as "Rail plus Property."

6
Implications for Asset Managers

We have introduced an array of factors that help explain the challenges facing public pension systems in the United States. It is important for asset managers who engage with pension systems to understand these dynamics. Understanding and anticipating client needs underpins successful investment mandates. This empathic approach to marketing is becoming increasingly important across all asset classes and specifically in financially and technically complex asset classes such as infrastructure, particularly as the investment management industry continues to evolve. As pension systems adopt increasingly customized investment models, asset managers need a more comprehensive understanding of their clients' balance sheet, portfolios, and cash flow requirements. This will facilitate more effective marketing and – for the larger investment managers – opportunities to offer solutions that incorporate varying levels of customization.

Certain sectors of the investment world have experienced outflows associated with the evolving pattern of institutional investing. Managers of traditional public equity and fixed income strategies have faced the dual pressures of alternative investment strategies (Figure 2.17) as well as index strategies. More recently, hedge fund managers have experienced redemptions for reasons of poor investment performance and high investment expenses. In general, increasing attention is being paid to expense issues, as we have discussed.

As illustrated (Figure 2.21) alternative investment strategies do not appear to have resulted in distinct portfolio benefits, perhaps for reasons we have posited. Consequently, managers of private capital strategies need to stay ahead of the curve on developments pertaining to their largest single client base, the public pension plans.

Finally, one of the persistent challenges facing the infrastructure investment management industry is the absence of a clear definition of what is meant by "infrastructure" investing. Steps have been taken to better define the asset class[126] but, as we have illustrated, there is insufficient benchmark data on infrastructure investments – whether gross or net of fees. Moreover, as with real estate investing, there is a wide risk/return gap between greenfield development projects and long-term availability-payment contracts. It is in the interests of the investment management industry to promote the development of defensible and empirically viable benchmarks. While asset managers seek to generate strong absolute returns and cash yield, the reality is that institutional investors like public pension funds need credible benchmarks to evaluate the performance of their portfolios. The absence of such benchmarks can easily deter pension funds from engaging with infrastructure as an asset class, certainly a missed opportunity.

Interestingly, one of the world's largest institutional investor, the Government Pension Fund Global (GPFG) of Norway, explored investing in private infrastructure in 2015 with the objective of obtaining access to diversifying return/risk properties and access to illiquidity premia. GPFG decided not to begin

---

[126]For example – as part of European Union Solvency II insurance regulations.

an infrastructure program at that time because the Norwegian government, through its Ministry of Finance, determined that the lack of data on private infrastructure makes it impossible to validate these two assertions.[127] It also cited political risk and potential reputational issues associated with necessarily large and potentially disruptive private infrastructure investments. Moreover, the Ministry stressed that the GPFG should not use its resources to promote developing market infrastructure or renewable energy.[128]

---

[127]It should be noted that GPFG investments in real estate are also undertaken without a concomitant benchmark, instead they are included within the tracking error of the fund's benchmark index.

[128]In October 2018, NBIM proposed including private renewable energy investments in the portfolio of GPFG, subject to (i) clearly defining the opportunity set, (ii) including this exposure in the fund's 1.25% deviation limit from its benchmark index, and (iii) undertaking these investments along with partners. For further detail, see Report to the Storting No. 23 (2015-2016) The Management of the Government Pension Fund in 2015 (unofficial English translation) and Letters to the Norwegian Ministry of Finance from Øystein Olsen (Governor of the Central Bank of Norway and Yngve Slyngstad (CEO of Norges Bank Investment Management) dated 10/29/18 and 12/20/2016.

7
Summary and Conclusions

This study examines the proposition that the public pension and infrastructure sectors can be better interconnected to harvest significant gains for both. Each is a "boiling frog" problem that has long been recognized and has now reached an inflection point in both public policy and business strategy. Underfunding of public pensions threatens promises made to beneficiaries and bondholders, fiscal integrity of government entities, and ultimately taxpayers. Pension asset allocation to infrastructure projects may hold promise as part of the solution. Meanwhile, underinvestment in the maintenance and development of infrastructure threatens a key element of future U.S. economic growth and depends on large applications of public or private capital. Infrastructure represents an attractive asset class for long-term institutional investors, notably pension systems. We address these twin issues jointly – supported by a broad public consensus that both must be addressed more effectively – and identify some of the key benefits and challenges.

There is an extensive literature on these issues and a host of arguments and policy solutions populate the debates. We start with data sourced directly from public filings of 25 public pension systems that account for more than half of all U.S. public pension liabilities and accrued assets. This set up an empirical basis for understanding the challenges facing administrators of public pension systems in the United States.[129] Pension math is

---

[129] All data quoted in this summary pertains exclusively to the pension

such that most inputs are exogenous to the control of pension administrators, highlighting the primacy of isolating those factors that can be influenced by decision-makers.

We note that 66% of revenues of the pension systems in our study have accrued from investment returns (22.5% are from employer contributions and the balance from employee contributions).

Discipline in funding employer contributions – a responsibility of government – is fundamental to sound pension administration. If discipline erodes, funding gaps follow. Making up this shortfall burdens fiscal budgets. Ultimately, pension solvency is a taxpayer responsibility and while some pension systems are particularly well-funded, others are approaching stress point.

Because of the limited weight of employee contributions as a source of funding, demographic changes – while significant – are of limited relevance. That said, it is instructive to observe that the ratio of active members to annuitants (excluding inactive participants) dropped to 1.4x in 2017 from 2.0x only a decade earlier, a factor that we illustrate is correlated to population growth and inter-regional demographics.

Benefit levels, with strong protections in law, have an obvious impact on pension solvency, and jurisdictions with richer benefits can be observed to have weaker funded status. But it is the area of portfolio management that demands attention – both because of the centrality of investment returns in pension funding and because the critical variable in determining pension liabilities is the expected future rate of investment performance, which determines the discount rate. We show a clear downward trend in pension discount rates, reflecting changing expectations

systems in our dataset.

for pension portfolio performance (from 7.9% in 2008 to 7.3% in 2017) even as the latter exceeds trailing 10-year returns.

Asset allocation, security selection, and aggressive management of investment expenses are the main factors available for pension administrators to influence pension solvency. Ideally, pension assets should be invested to match liabilities and cash flows, but that is highly complex and atypical in the U.S. public pension system.

Seeking superior returns, pension systems have slowly diversified away from traditional equities and fixed income (83.7% of portfolios in 2008 and 71.7% in 2017) towards alternative investments. This approach is not uniform as some public pension systems have very little exposure to alternative investments while others have even begun unwinding such exposure. We found no evidence of correlation between alternative asset allocation and net investment returns. We postulate that this may be the result of strong market beta over the decade ending 2017, the effect of fees paid to obtain alternative exposures, and the challenges of selecting the best investment managers and funds.

In light of the importance of investment expenses, it is noteworthy that fee disclosure is quite limited and that comparability between pension systems is almost impossible. We posit that investment expenses for the 25 largest pension systems may be $18 billion a year - about 11% of annual pension benefit payments. With due cause, treasurers in several states have made containment of investment expenses a campaign issue.

We build on the public pension discussion by focusing on the role of infrastructure investing. We illustrate that investing in this asset class remains at a nascent stage in the United States. The average portfolio allocation of the public pension system in our dataset to infrastructure is about 1%.

Pension systems articulate several reasons for investing in infrastructure, and we illustrate using a market index that the asset class provides diversification, stable cash flows, and strong risk-adjusted returns. The data do not confirm the hypothesis of inflation protection.

We show that the way in which pension systems invest in infrastructure has yielded returns from capital appreciation through private equity-style funds – which may nevertheless prove to be unsustainable due to rising valuations in the absence of increased deal flow. But this mode of investing is not targeted to the investment objectives that pensions systems articulate when entering this asset class. Investing through open-end funds or on a direct basis would be more appropriate to such objectives, alongside closed-end funds that provide upside from capital appreciation.

We argue that pension system governance can be enhanced through including more trustees with investing, finance, and actuarial experience, greater discipline in funding employer contributions, better transparency in the determination of pension benefits, greater attention by the taxpayer to all aspects of pension funding, more uniformity in determination of expected investment returns, liability and cash flow-sensitive investment management, and enhanced expense reporting along with active management of investment expenses.

Part of the solution lies in revisiting the relationship between pension systems and the investment managers who serve them. Pension systems can obtain greater control over exposures and expenses along a continuum that includes co-investing, customization, collaboration with peers, jointly-owned or captive investment affiliates, and direct investing.

We also argue that – exemplified by the Canadian public pension systems, for example – infrastructure should become more central to pension portfolios. But this requires an increased supply of deals – likely through public-private partnerships and other greenfield or repurposed brownfield investing. For this to occur, public-private partnerships need to become a more widely accepted form of project delivery, something that is not yet evident in the United States. Such activity can lead to a virtuous circle between the long-duration nature of pension assets and the long-term financing needs of infrastructure development. We acknowledge however that structural challenges abound in the U.S. context.

Finally, we propose that investment managers would do well to adopt a more empathic approach to understanding their most important clients, pension funds. Those able to, should consider offering investing solutions that directly address the cash flow and balance sheet needs of public pension investors. Even then, they may not preempt challenges to the intermediary model of investing, with pension funds creating direct investment capabilities, as some foreign pension funds and sovereign wealth funds have done with some success.

Appendix – Description of Indexes

- **MSCI Global Infrastructure Index**. Measures investment performance of infrastructure assets. Time-weighted return methodology for equity-based investments across the world. Valuation-based return index, valuations based on appraisal methodology not transactional based methodology. Return profile split into distributed income and capital return. Index reflects "true" returns, purged of exchange rate effects. Index is segmented by investment styles. Quarterly frequency.

- **Dow Jones Brookfield Global Infrastructure Composite Index**. Measures performance of pure-play infrastructure companies domiciled globally. The index covers all sectors of the infrastructure market and includes Master Limited Partnerships in addition to other equity securities. To be included in the index, a company must derive at least 70% of its cash flows from infrastructure lines of business.

- **MSCI Global Quarterly Property Fund Index**. Measures unlevered total returns of directly held standing property investments.

- **MSCI IPD Global Quarterly Property Fund Index**. Measures the performance of property funds and their underlying assets, globally diversified.

- **S&P U.S. REIT Index**. Measures the investable universe of publicly traded real estate investment trusts domiciled in the United States.

- **Cambridge Associates Buyout & Growth Equity Index**. Measures fund-level performance data drawn from the quarterly and audited annual financial statements of private equity fund managers, net of all fees.

- **Dow Jones Commodity Index**. Measures the commodity futures market emphasizing diversification and liquidity through a simple, straightforward, equal-weighted approach.

- **HFRX Aggregate Index**. Equally weighted index across all sub-strategy and regional hedge fund indices, net of all fees.

- **MSCI All Country World Index**. A free float-adjusted market capitalization weighted equity index that includes both emerging and developed world markets.

- **Bloomberg Barclays Global-Aggregate Total Return Index**. Flagship measure of global investment grade debt from twenty-four local currency markets, includes treasury, government-related, corporate and securitized fixed-rate bonds from both developed and emerging market issuers.

- **S&P U.S. Treasury Bond Current 10-year Index**. A one-security index comprising the most recently issued 10-year U.S. Treasury note or bond.

- **U.S. CPI Urban Consumers**. Measures prices paid by consumers for a market basket of consumer goods and services.

References

1. The Big Squeeze: How Money Managers' Fees Crush State Budgets And Workers Retirement Hopes. Washington, DC: American Federation of Teachers (AFT) (2017).

2. Andonov, Aleksandar and Hochberg, Yael V. and Rauh, Joshua D., Political Representation and Governance: Evidence from the Investment Decisions of Public Pension Funds (November 16, 2017). Journal of Finance, Forthcoming. Available at SSRN: https://ssrn.com/abstract=2754820 or http://dx.doi.org/10.2139/ssrn.2754820.

3. Andonov, Aleksandar and Kraeussl, Roman and Rauh, Joshua D., The Subsidy to Infrastructure as an Asset Class (May 2019). Stanford University Graduate School of Business Research Paper No. 18-42. Available at SSRN: https://ssrn.com/abstract=3245543 or http://dx.doi.org/10.2139/ssrn.3245543

4. Anson, Mark J.P., A Discount Rate for Public Pension Plans (December 1, 2011). Journal of Investment Consulting, Vol. 12, No. 2, pp. 16-22, 2011. Available at SSRN: https://ssrn.com/abstract=2004610.

5. Aubry, Jean-Pierre, Crawford, Caroline V. and Wandrei, Kevin, Stability in Overall Pension Plan Funding Masks a Growing Divide. Center for State & Local Government Excellence, Washington, DC, October 2018.

6. Beermann, Jack Michael, The Public Pension Crisis (September 23, 2012). Washington & Lee Law Review,

Vol. 70, No. 1; Boston Univ. School of Law, Public Law Research Paper No. 12-48. Available at SSRN: `https://ssrn.com/abstract=2131481` or `http://dx.doi.org/10.2139/ssrn.2131481`

7. Bennon, Michael and Monk, Ashby H. B. and Cho, YJ, In-Kind Infrastructure Investments by Public Pensions: The Queensland Motorways Case Study (June 5, 2017). Stanford Global Projects Center, June 5, 2017. Available at SSRN: `https://ssrn.com/abstract=2981707` or `http://dx.doi.org/10.2139/ssrn.2981707`.

8. Bennon, Michael, Monk, Ashby, and Nowacki, Caroline, Dutch Pensions Paving the Way for Infrastructure Development (Spring 2015). The Journal of Structured Finance.

9. Brainard, Keith and Brown, Alex, Significant Reforms to State Retirement Systems (June 2016). National Association of State Retirement Administrators.

10. California State Teachers Retirement System, 2017 Annual Investment Cost Report (January 30, 2019).

11. Chen, Gang and Matkin, David S. T., Actuarial Inputs and the Valuation of Public Pension Liabilities and Contribution Requirements: A Simulation Approach (Spring 2017). Public Budgeting & Finance, Vol. 37, Issue 1, pp. 68-87, 2017. Available at SSRN: `https://ssrn.com/abstract=2929404` or `http://dx.doi.org/10.1111/pbaf.12154`

12. Clark, Gordon L. and Monk, Ashby H. B. and Orr, Ryan and Scott, William, The New Era of Infrastructure Investing (May 10, 2011). Available at SSRN: `https://ssrn.com/abstract=1837813` or `http://dx.doi.org/10.2139/ssrn.1837813`

13. Cooper, Donna and Craig, John F. Using Pension Funds to Build Infrastructure and Put Americans to Work. Washington, DC: Center for American Progress (March 2013).

14. Dachis, Benjamin, New and Improved: How Institutional Investment in Public Infrastructure can Benefit Taxpayers and Consumers (March 28, 2017). C.D. Howe Institute Commentary 473. Available at SSRN: `https://ssrn.com/abstract=2942903` or `http://dx.doi.org/10.2139/ssrn.2942903`

15. Ely, Danielle M. and Hamilton, Brady E. Trends in fertility and mother's age at first birth among rural and metropolitan counties: United States, 2007–2017. NCHS Data Brief, no 323. Hyattsville, MD: National Center for Health Statistics. 2018.

16. Kellar, Elizabeth, Understanding Public Pensions: A Guide for Elected Officials, Washington, DC: Center for State & Local Governance Excellence (April 2017)

17. Mattoon, Rick, Issues Facing State and Local Government Pensions. Economic Perspectives, Vol. 31, No. 3, 2007. Available at SSRN: `https://ssrn.com/abstract=1012418`

18. Mitchell, Olivia S. and Yang, Tongxuan, Public Pension Governance, Funding, and Performance: A Longitudinal Appraisal (2005). Pension Research Council WP2005-2. Available at SSRN: `https://ssrn.com/abstract=755045` or `http://dx.doi.org/10.2139/ssrn.755045`

19. Monahan, Amy, Public Pension Plan Reform: The Legal Framework (March 17, 2010). Education, Finance & Policy, Vol. 5, 2010; Minnesota Legal Studies Research No. 10-13. Available at SSRN: `https://ssrn.com/abstract=1573864`

20. Monk, A. H. B. and Sharma, R. and Feng, W., Social Capital and Building an Institutional Investor's Collaborative Network (November 29, 2015). Available at SSRN: `https://ssrn.com/abstract=2698178` or `http://dx.doi.org/10.2139/ssrn.2698178`

21. Munnell, Alicia H. and Aubry, Jean-Pierre, The Funding of State and Local Pensions: 2015-2020 (June 2016). Center for Retirement Research at Boston College.

22. Munnell, Alicia H., Aubry, Jean-Pierre, and Hurwitz, Josh, How Sensitive is Public Pension Funding to Investment Returns? (September 2013), Center for Retirement Research at Boston College.

23. Munnell, Alicia H, Aubry, Jean-Pierre, and Cafarelli, Mark, How Did State/Local Plans Become Underfunded? (January 2015), Center for Retirement Research at Boston College.

24. NASRA Issue Brief: Employee Contributions to Public Pension Plans (October 2018). National Association of State Retirement Administrators.

25. Novy-Marx, Robert and Rauh, Joshua D., Public Pension Promises: How Big are They and What are They Worth? (October 8, 2010). Journal of Finance, Forthcoming. Available at SSRN: `https://ssrn.com/abstract=1352608` or `http://dx.doi.org/10.2139/ssrn.1352608`.

26. Offerman, Douglas, Porter, Lauren, Laskey, Amy, Raphael, Richard: Enhancing the Analysis of U.S. State and Local Government Pension Obligations (February 17, 2011). Fitch Ratings.

27. Ososami, Oladunni M. and Tauzer, Todd N. For the Five Highest- Funded U.S. State Plans, Being Proactive Keeps

Liabilities Manageable (October 24, 2017). S&P Global Ratings.

28. Park, Youngkyun, Public Pension Plan Allocations, Washington, DC: Employee Benefits Research Institute Notes Vol 30, No. 4 (April 2009).

29. Pennsylvania Treasury, Public Pension Management and Asset Investment Review Commission of the State of Pennsylvania, Final Report and Recommendations, First Printing (December 19, 2018).

30. Tauzer, Todd N. and Kanaster, Todd D., Looking Forward: The Application of The Discount Rate in Funding U.S. Government Pensions (September 13, 2018). S&P Global Ratings.

31. Weinberg, Sheila and Norcross, Eileen, GASB 67 and GASB 68: What the New Accounting Standards Mean for Public Pension Reporting (June 2017), Mercatus Center at George Mason University.

About the Authors

Clive Lipshitz

Clive Lipshitz is managing partner of Tradewind Interstate Advisors where he consults to institutional investors, alternative investment management firms, and other entities. He is also a guest scholar at New York University Stern School of Business.

Mr. Lipshitz has extensive experience in investment portfolio strategy and in the development and marketing of alternative investment products and solutions to institutional investors, particularly in the area of real assets. He established and for many years managed the strategy and product development function for Credit Suisse Asset Management, a position he later played at Brookfield Asset Management. In these roles, he developed more than 30 new investment businesses.

Earlier in his career, he was a growth capital investor at TDA Capital Partners and in the Office of the Chairman at PaineWebber.

Recently, Mr. Lipshitz has advised corporations and institutions such as The Carlyle Group, AECOM, and the NYU Marron Institute of Urban Management on investment product marketing and on infrastructure finance and policy. He has authored academic studies on public pension systems at Stanford's Institute for Economic Policy Research and at NYU.

Mr. Lipshitz has extensive global experience, having worked

131

in Brazil, Mexico, Canada, the UK, Switzerland, Israel, South Africa, India, Singapore, and Hong Kong.

Ingo Walter

Ingo Walter has been based almost all of his professional career at New York University, including periods of residency at Insead, the University of Mannheim, the Institute for Southeast Asian Studies in Singapore, the free University of Berlin, IESE in Spain, the University of Western Australia, and others.

At NYU he has chaired several academic departments, directed the Salomon Center for the Study of Financial Institutions for thirteen years, and served two four-year terms as Vice Dean for Academic Affairs and more recently Dean of Faculty.

His early academic and advisory work focused on international trade policy, notably the impact of tariffs and non-tariff barriers on developing country trade and growth. This led to work on trade and the natural environment - how environmental policy developments can be built into the generally accepted models of global production in a book titled "The International Economics of Pollution" (MacMillan, 1974)- and in a Rockefeller Foundation - Bellagio conference volume on international trade in garbage. A bit later he focused on non-market constraints facing foreign direct investment in a co-authored volume "Multinationals Under Fire" (John Wiley, 1980), which covered many of the ESG concerns widely discussed today.

The focus on trade and investment led to a research focus on market-access in the financial services industry, and an effort to understand the structure, conduct and performance of its main functional pillars - commercial banking, securities, insurance and asset management - in all their complexity. The work had both strategic and public policy dimensions, including systemic and firm-specific risk management and problems that surfaced in the financial crisis in 2007-08. This included two volumes by NYU faculty teams on crisis forensics and remediation in search of a sustainable balance between global financial efficiency and stability.

Currently Prof. Walter is engaged in a multi-disciplinary study of infrastructure finance, and is extending his work on reputational risk.

Ingo Walter has served on a number of boards - currently the Board of Directors of the National Bureau of Economic Research - and has advised various financial firms and government agencies.

About the Infrastructure Finance Initiative

This book is a product of the NYU Stern Infrastructure Finance Initiative. This Initiative centers on policy-relevant academic research and education in infrastructure finance, comprising three areas of activity: (a) Generating and disseminating of insights in the form of targeted publications, (b) Convening outreach conferences and symposia on infrastructure finance and participation in such activities elsewhere, and (c) Creating of a serious teaching capability at NYU Stern and other institutions in the form of course development and case-writing on project and infrastructure finance. The objective is to create a resource in the academic, policymaking and business communities that is useful and creative in the realm of infrastructure finance. The NYU Stern Infrastructure Finance Initiative has been supported by a multi-year grant from the New York University Global Institute for Advanced Study. For further details, please contact Ingo Walter, Director, NYU Stern Infrastructure Finance Initiative.